Contents

Use What You Know

Getting Ready Numbers to 10

Exploring Addition Sums to 6

Exploring Subtraction Differences to 6

Addition Strategies

Subtraction Strategies

Shapes and Patterns

Place Value Numbers to 100

Addition and Subtraction to 12

Measurement and Fractions

Time and Money

Exploring Addition and Subtraction of 2-Digit Numbers

Addition and Subtraction to 18

Name ________________________________

1.1
USE WHAT YOU KNOW

Sorting by Color and Size

Cut and paste.
Put in the object that belongs.

1.

2.

3.

4.

Visual Thinking

5. Where does the [bow tie] belong? Ring the group.

Use with text pages 3–4.

Name ____________________

1.2 USE WHAT YOU KNOW

Patterns

Ring to continue the pattern.

1.

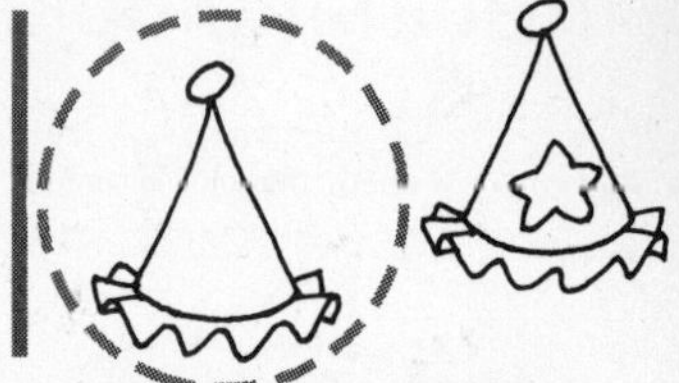

2.

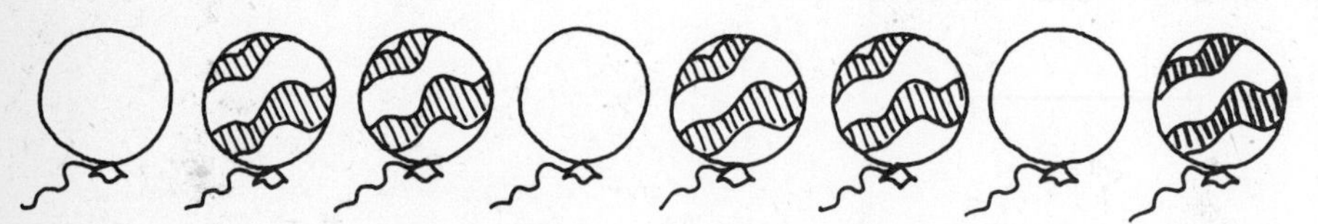

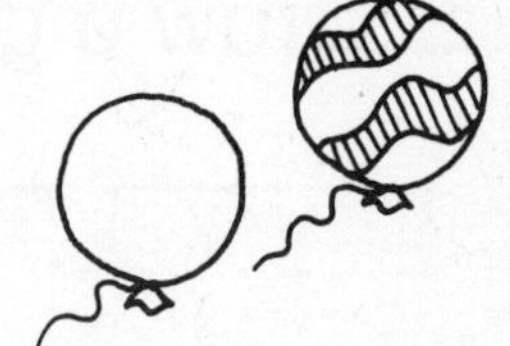

3.

4.

Reasoning

5. Which patterns are alike?
Ring them.

A B A B A B　　　　A B B A B B

A B B A B B　　　　A A A A A A

Use with text pages 5–6.

Name ____________________

1.3 USE WHAT YOU KNOW

Same, More, Fewer

1. Draw a group that has the same number.

2. Draw a group that has more.

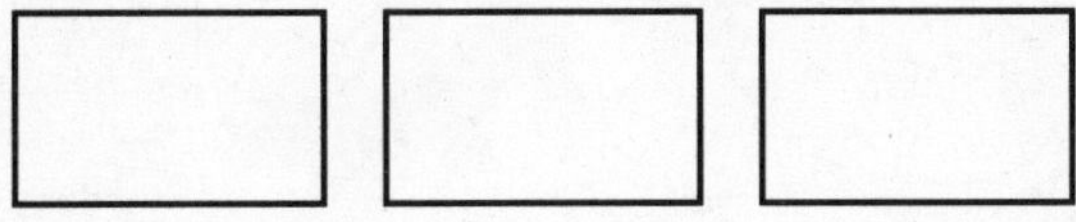

3. Draw a group that has 1 more.

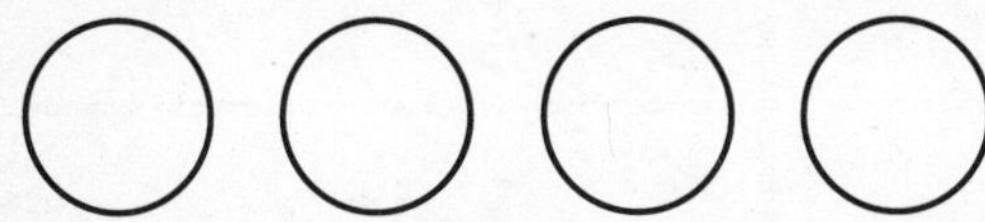

4. Draw a group that has fewer.

Number Sense

5. Which group has more?
Ring the group.

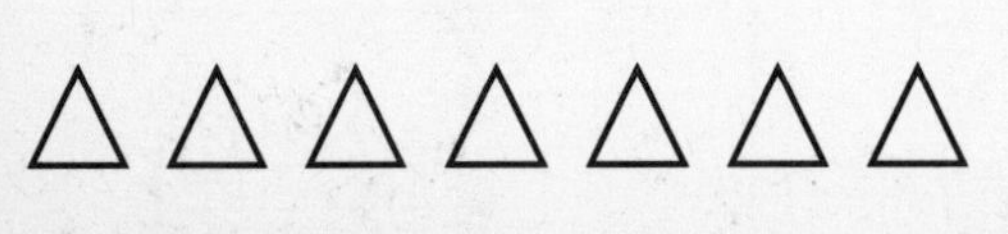

Use with text pages 7–8.

Name ______________________________

Two, One, Three

1.4
USE WHAT YOU KNOW

Ring each pair.

Put a counter on each bird.
Write how many.

1.

2

2.

3.

Number Sense

4. Which shows 1 more than a pair? Ring the group.

Use with text pages 9–10.

Name ______________________

Four and Five

Write how many.

1.

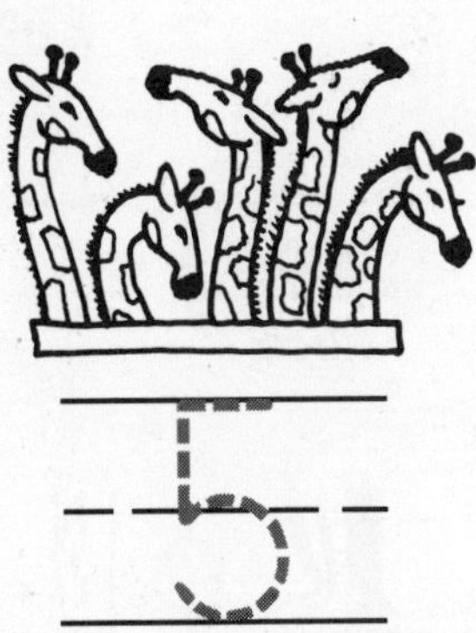

5

2.

3.

Number Sense

4. Ring the group that has more than 3.
Draw an X on the groups that have the same number.

Use with text pages 11–12.

Name ______________________________

1.6 USE WHAT YOU KNOW

Counting Pennies

Write how much.

1.

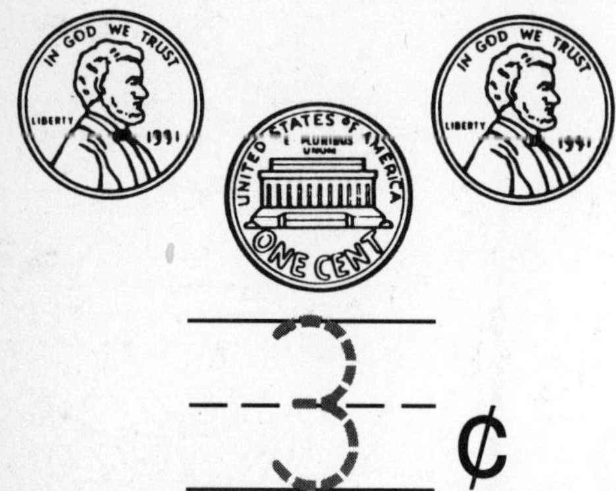

3 ¢

2.

____ ¢

3.

____ ¢

4.

____ ¢

5.

____ ¢

6.

____ ¢

Number Sense

7. Look at each purse. Ring the purse that has more pennies. Draw an X on the purse that has fewer pennies.

Use with text pages 13–14.

Name ______________________

1.7 USE WHAT YOU KNOW

Zero

Write 0.

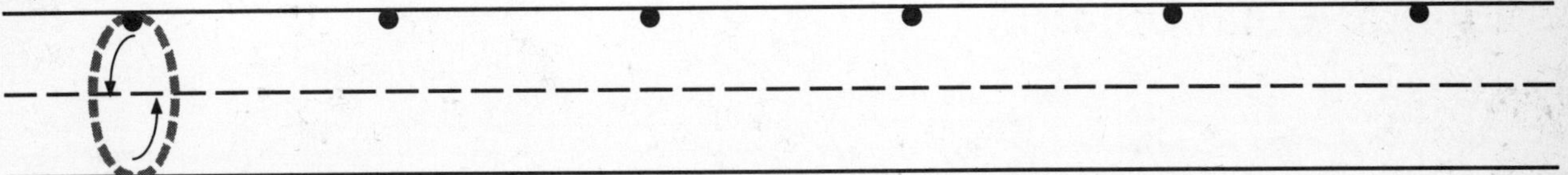

Write how many.

1.

2.

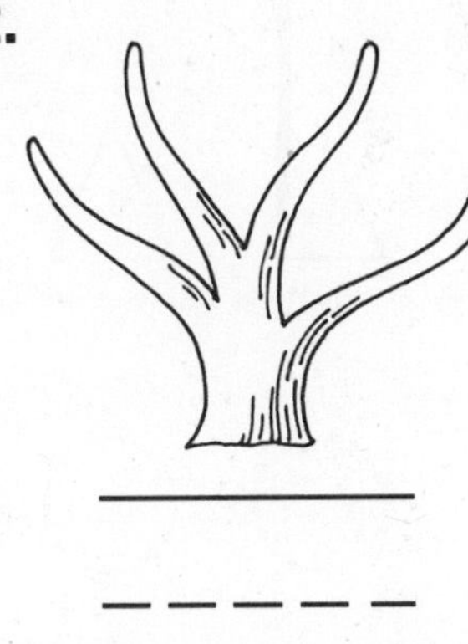

3.

4.

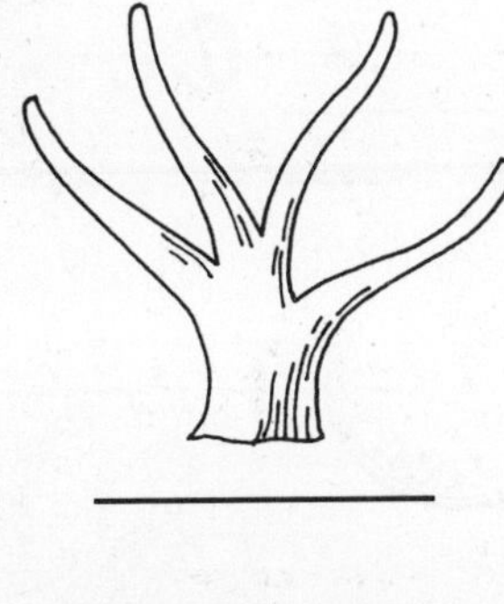

5.

6.

Number Sense

7. Ring the group that has more than 4.
Draw an X on the groups that have the same number.

Name ____________________

1.8 USE WHAT YOU KNOW

Problem-Solving Strategy

Draw a Picture

Continue each pattern.

1.

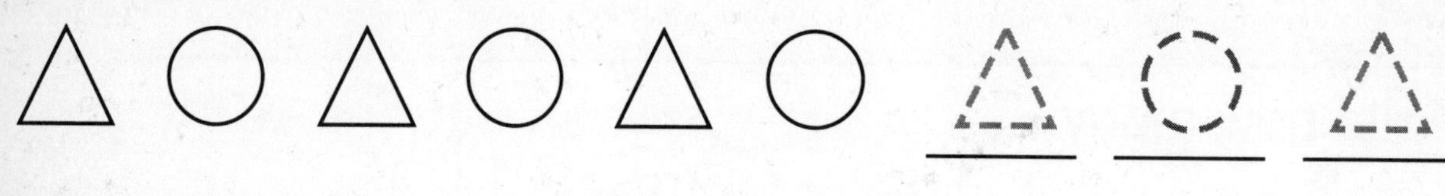

2.

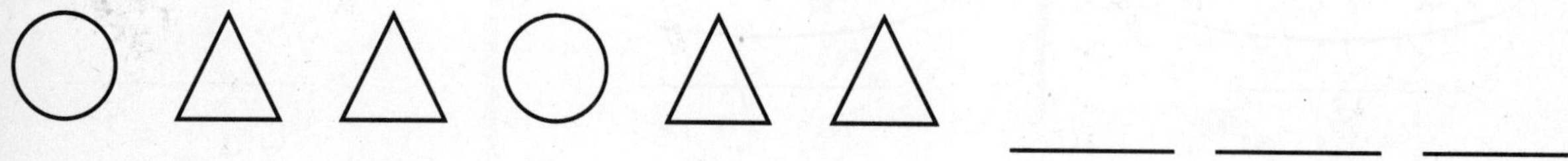

3.

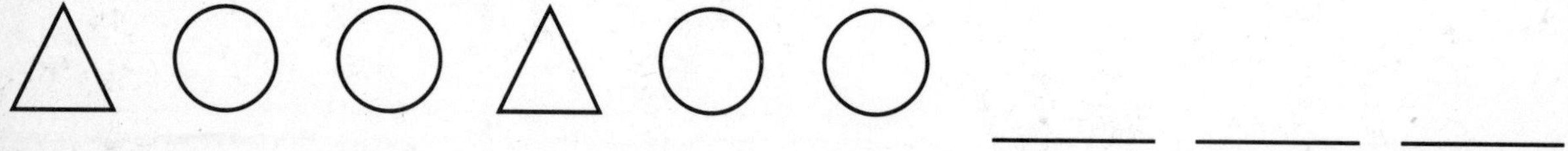

4.

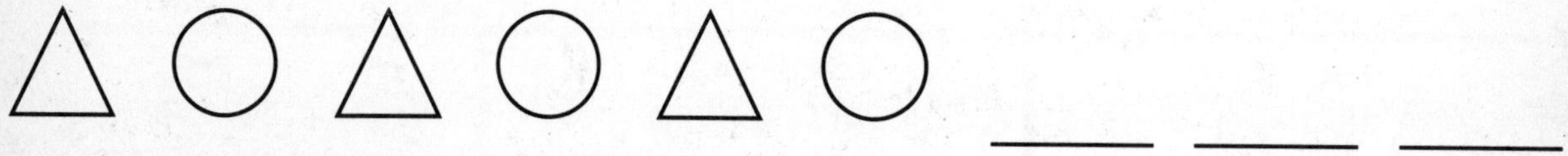

5.

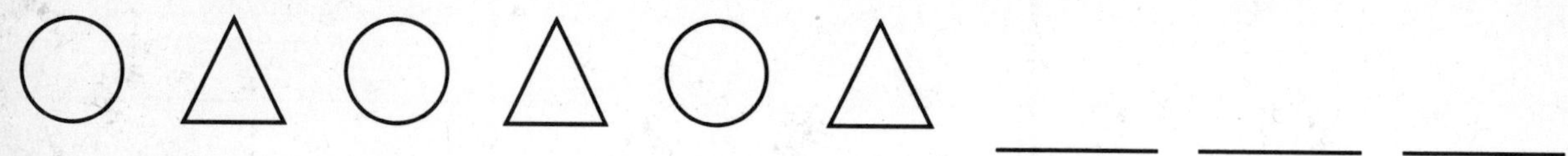

6.

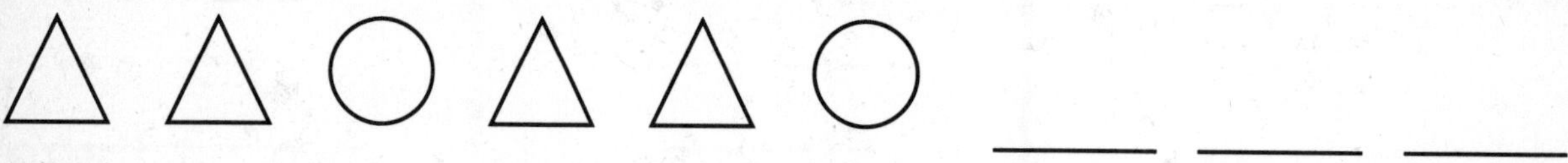

7.

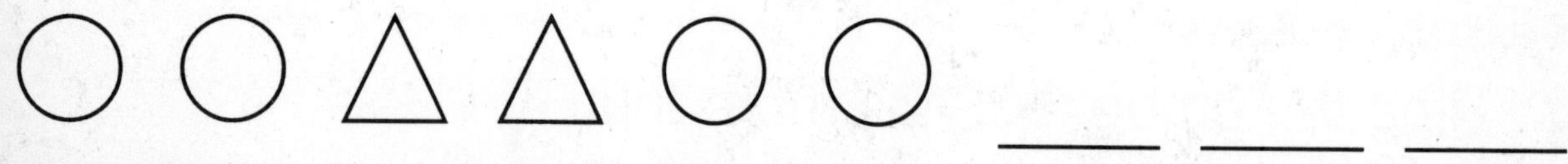

Reasoning

8. Do rows 3 and 6 show the same pattern? Ring **Yes** or **No**.

Yes No

Name ____________________

1.9
USE WHAT YOU KNOW

Six and Seven

Write how many. Ring the number word.

1.

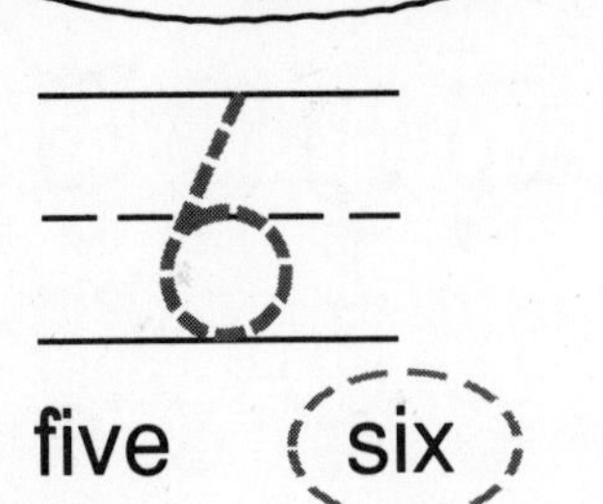

five (six)

2.

four five

3.

zero one

4.

five six

5.

six seven

6.

two three

Visual Thinking

7. Ring the groups that have more than 5.
Draw an X on the groups that have fewer than 5.

5

Name ___

USE WHAT YOU KNOW

Eight and Nine

Which groups have 8? Ring them red.

1.

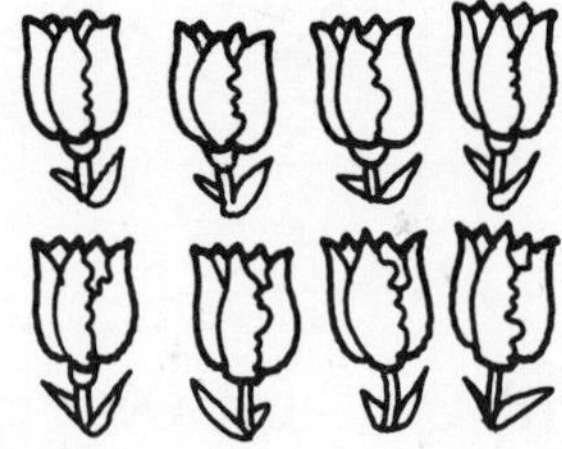

Which groups have 9? Ring them blue.

2.

Number Sense

3. Ring the group that has more.

Use with text pages 23–24.

Name ________________________________

1.11
USE WHAT YOU KNOW

Ten

Ring how many. Then write the number.

1. 

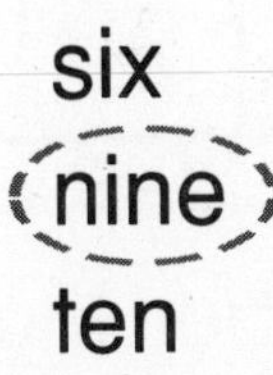

six
nine
ten

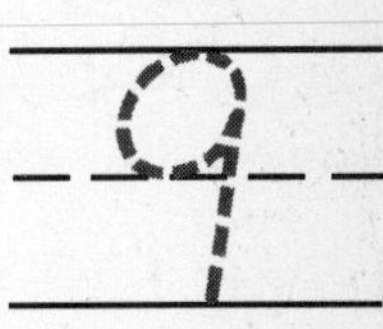

2.

five
six
seven

3.

ten
zero
two

4.

eight
three
one

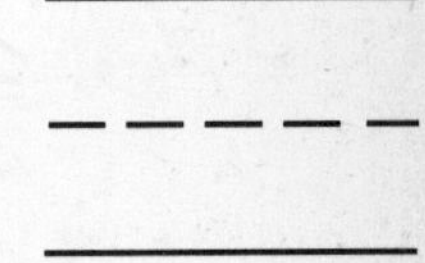

Reasoning

5. Which group of dolphins has 2 fewer than 9?
Ring the group.

Name ______________________________

1.12
USE WHAT YOU KNOW

Order Through 10

Write the number that comes next.

1. 3, 4, 5

2. 4, 5, ____

3. 8, 9, ____

4. 5, 6, ____

5. 0, 1, ____

6. 2, 3, ____

Count backward. Write the missing numbers.

7. 10, 9, ____, ____, ____, 5, 4, ____, 2, ____, 0

8. 10, ____, ____, 7, 6, ____, ____, ____, ____, 1

Number Sense

9. Ring the group that comes next.

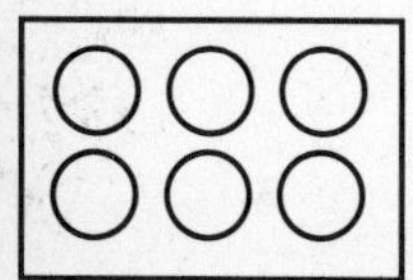

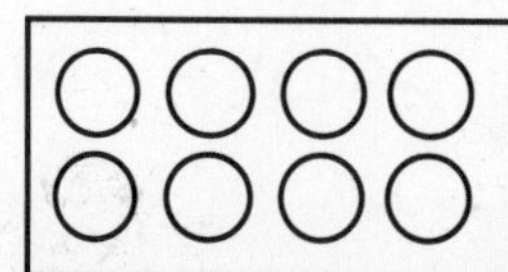

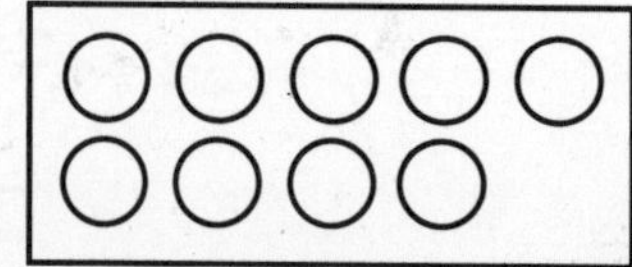

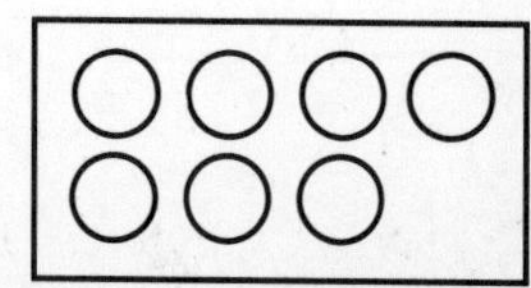

Use with text pages 27–28.

Name ______________________________

1.13

USE WHAT YOU KNOW

Comparing Numbers

Write how many.
Then ring the number that is greater.

1.

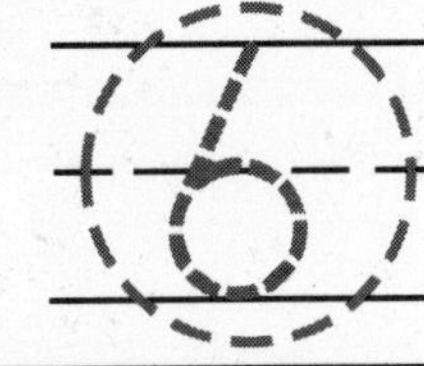
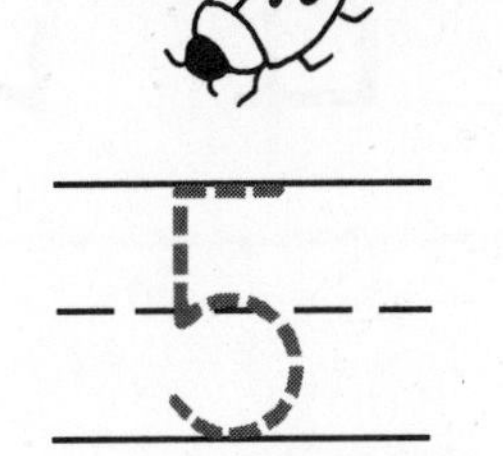

6 ______ 5 ______

2.

______ ______

Write how many.
Then ring the number that is less.

3.

______ ______

4.

______ ______

Story Corner

Complete the sentences. Use these words.

six **ten**

5. Ten is greater than ______ .

6. Six is less than ______ .

Use with text pages 29–30.

Name ____________________

1.14 USE WHAT YOU KNOW

Problem-Solving Strategy

Make a Pictograph

1. Count each shape.
   Draw shapes to complete the graph.

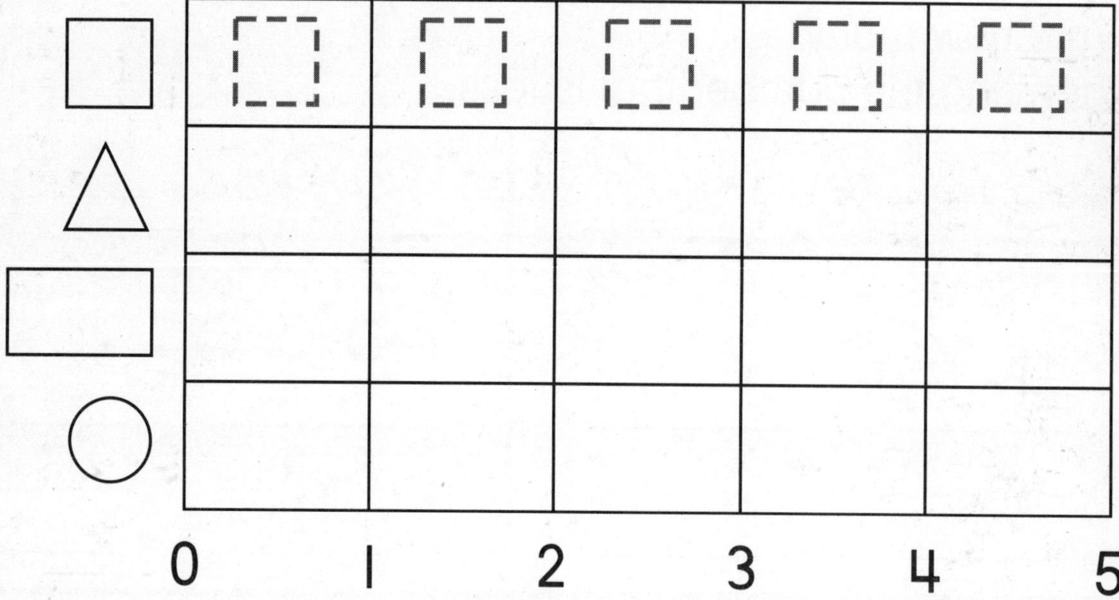

Reasoning

Look at the graph.

2. Ring the one with more.

 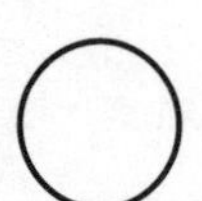

3. Ring the one with fewer.

 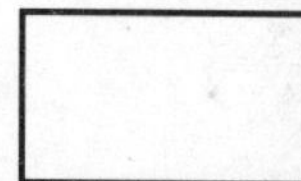

Use with text pages 31–32.

Name ____________________

2.1 USE WHAT YOU KNOW

Understanding Addition

Tell a story to a friend. Write how many.

How many? How many join? How many in all?

1.

4

1

5

2.

____

____

____

3.

____

____

____

Problem Solving

Make up a story. Write how many in all.

4.

____

5.

____

Use with text pages 41–42.

Name ______________________

2.2
USE WHAT YOU KNOW

Addition Sentences

Write the addition sentences.

1.

2 + 1 = 3

2.

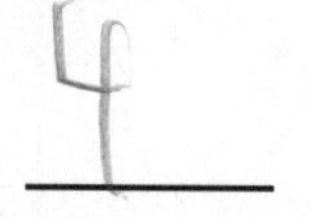

4 + 2 = 4

3.

4 + 1 = 5

4.

3 + 2 = 5

5.

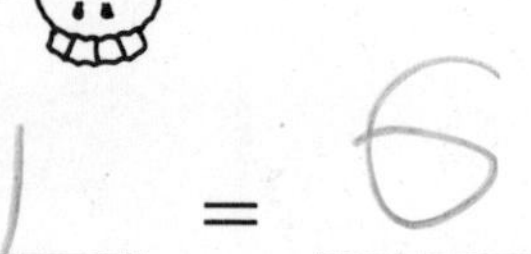

5 + 1 = 6

6.

1 + 2 = 3

Story Corner

7. Tell a story to a friend. Write an addition sentence.

2 + 2 = 4

Use with text pages 43–44.

Name ______________________________

2.3
USE WHAT YOU KNOW

Order in Addition

Use counters.
Draw X to show how many.
Write the sum.

1.

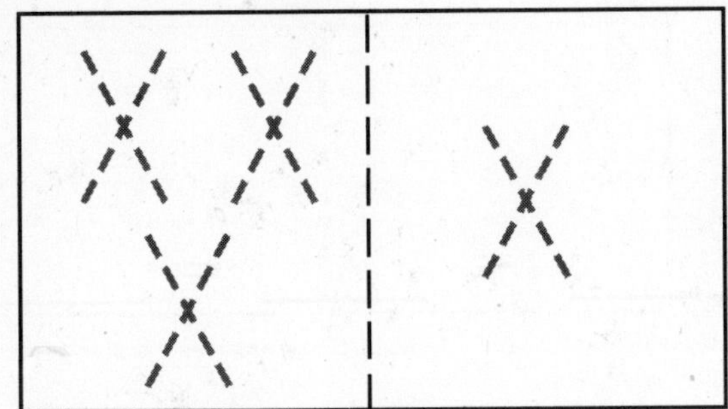

$3 + 1 =$ 4

$1 + 3 =$ 4

2.

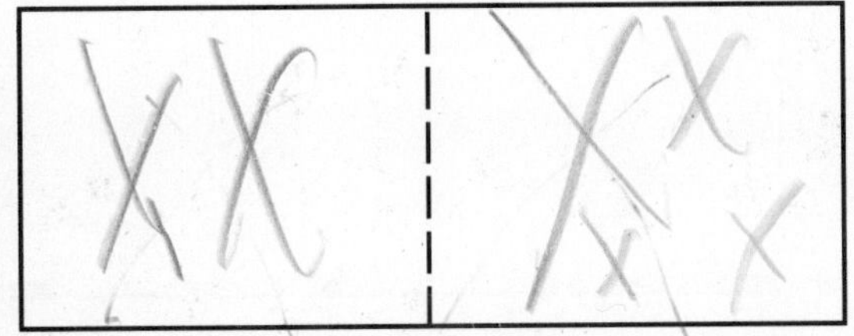

$2 + 4 =$ 6

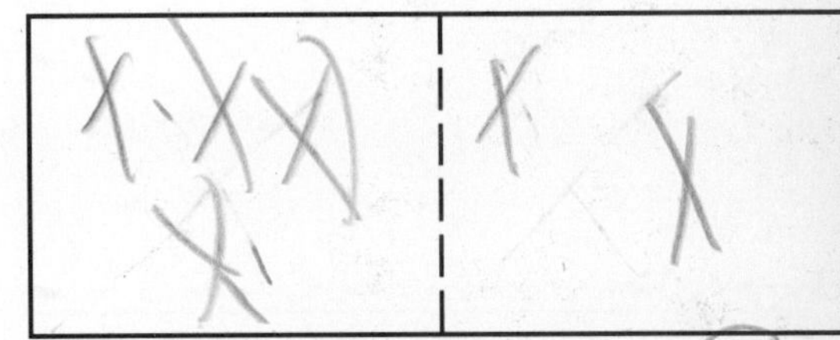

$4 + 2 =$ 6

3.

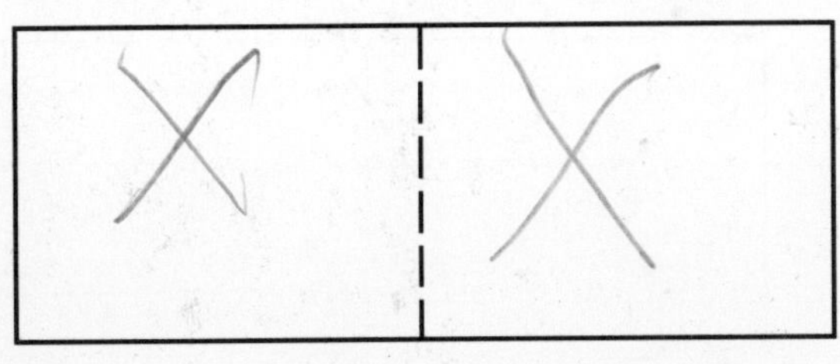

$4 + 1 =$ 5

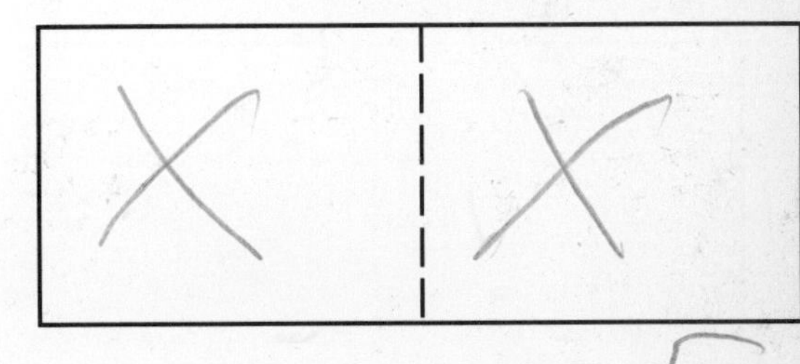

$1 + 4 =$ 5

Reasoning

4. Ring the pair that shows the same number.

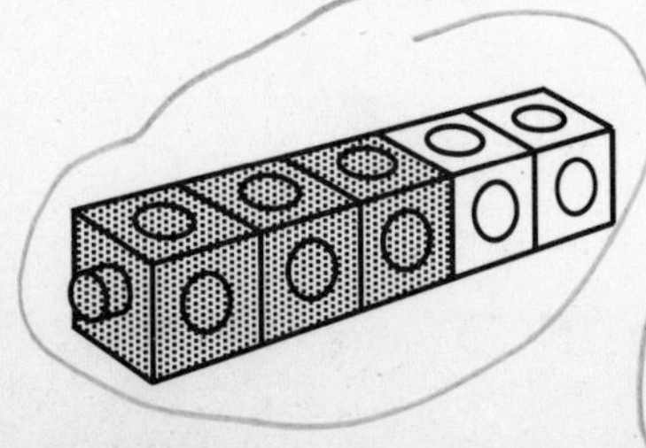

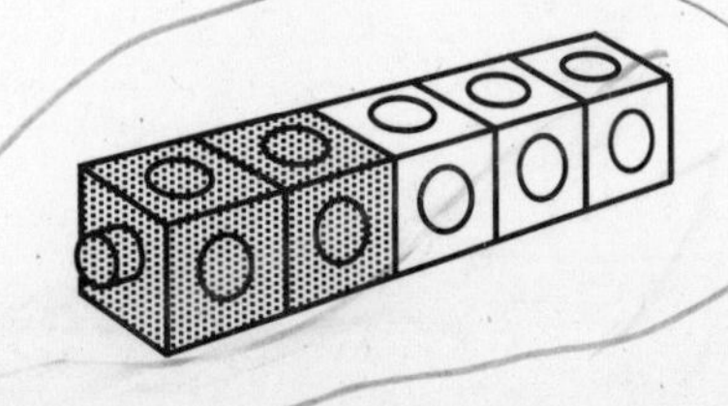

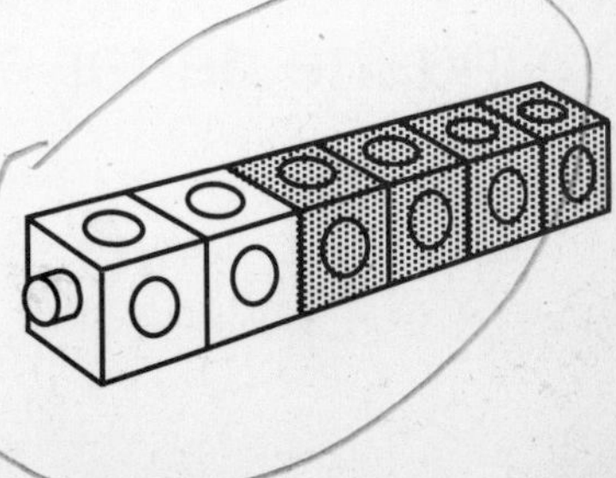

Name ______________________________

2.4
USE WHAT YOU KNOW

Adding 0

Use counters.
Draw dots to show how many.
Write the sum.

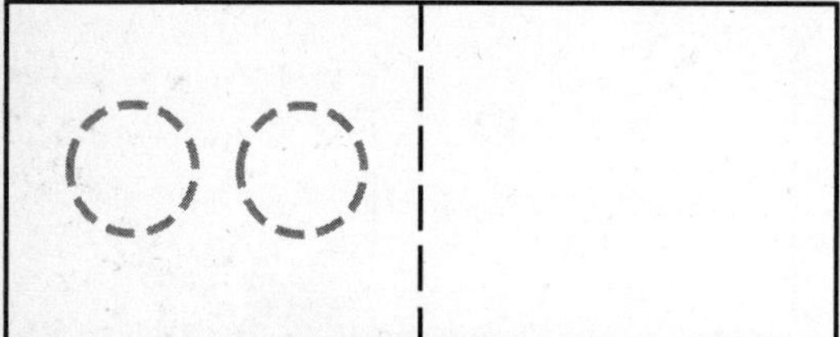

$2 + 0 = \underline{2}$

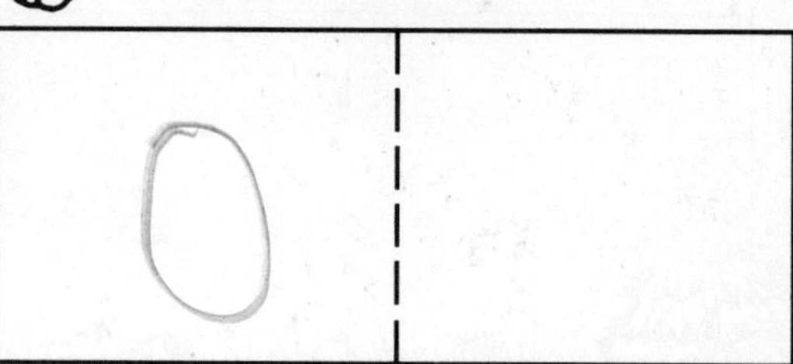

$0 + 3 = \underline{\quad}$

3.

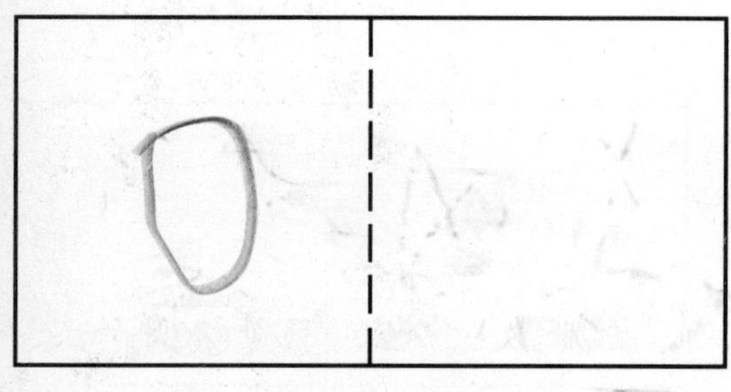

$0 + 5 = \underline{\quad}$

4.

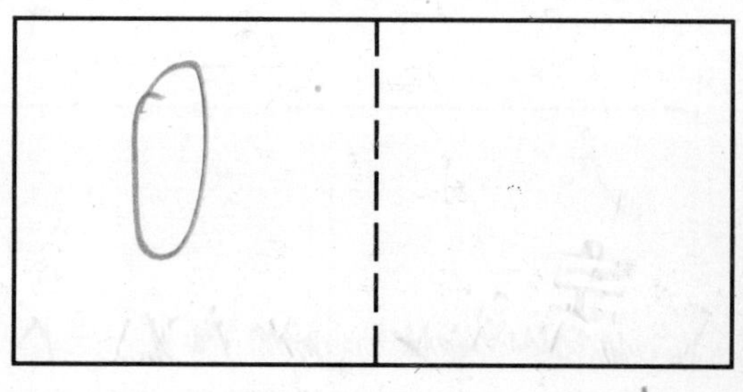

$1 + 0 = \underline{\quad}$

5.

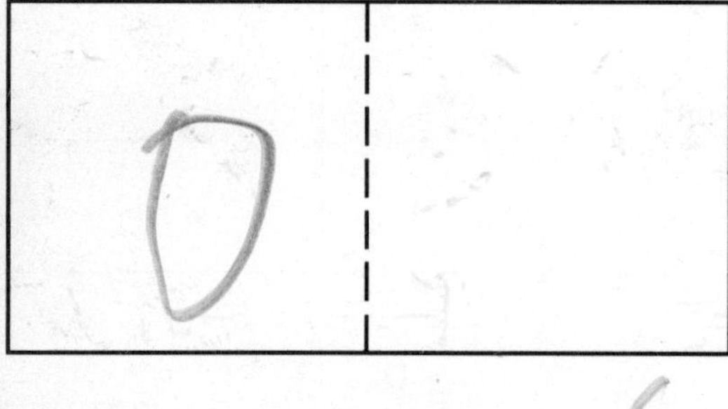

$6 + 0 = \underline{\quad}$

6.

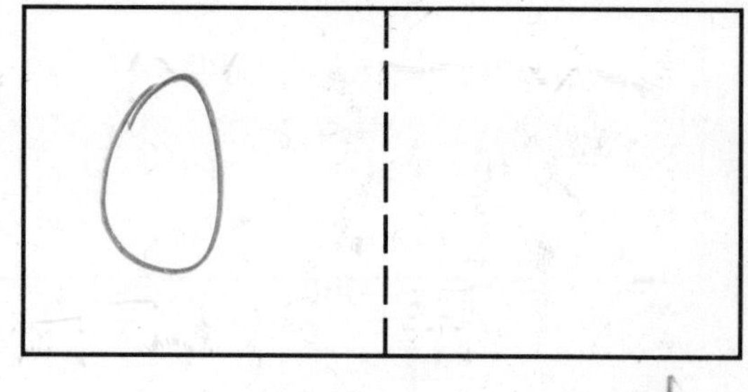

$0 + 4 = \underline{\quad}$

Number Sense

7. Ring the better estimate.

$4 + 0 = \underline{\ ?\ }$

greater than 5

less than 5

Use with text pages 47–48.

Name ___________________________

2.5
USE WHAT YOU KNOW

Problem-Solving Strategy

Draw a Picture

Make up a story.
Complete the picture. Solve.

1.

$2 + 1 =$ 3

2.

$3 + 2 =$ 5

3.

$5 + 1 =$ 6

Reasoning

4. Continue the pattern.

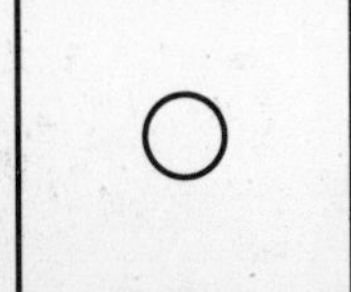 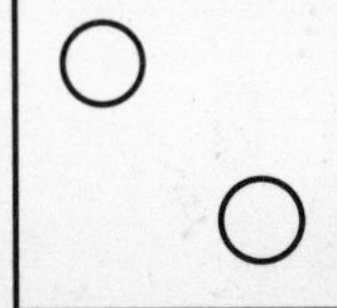 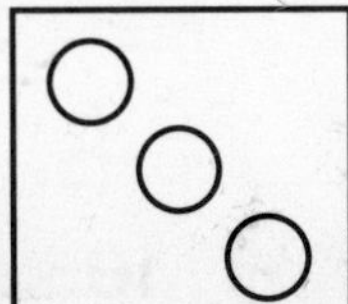 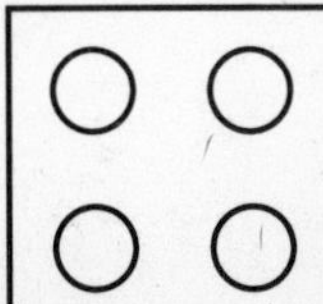 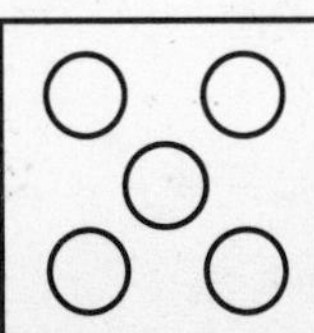 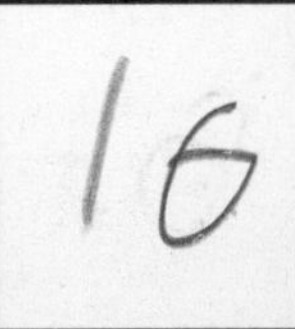

Name ______________________________

2.6
USE WHAT YOU KNOW

Addition Combinations

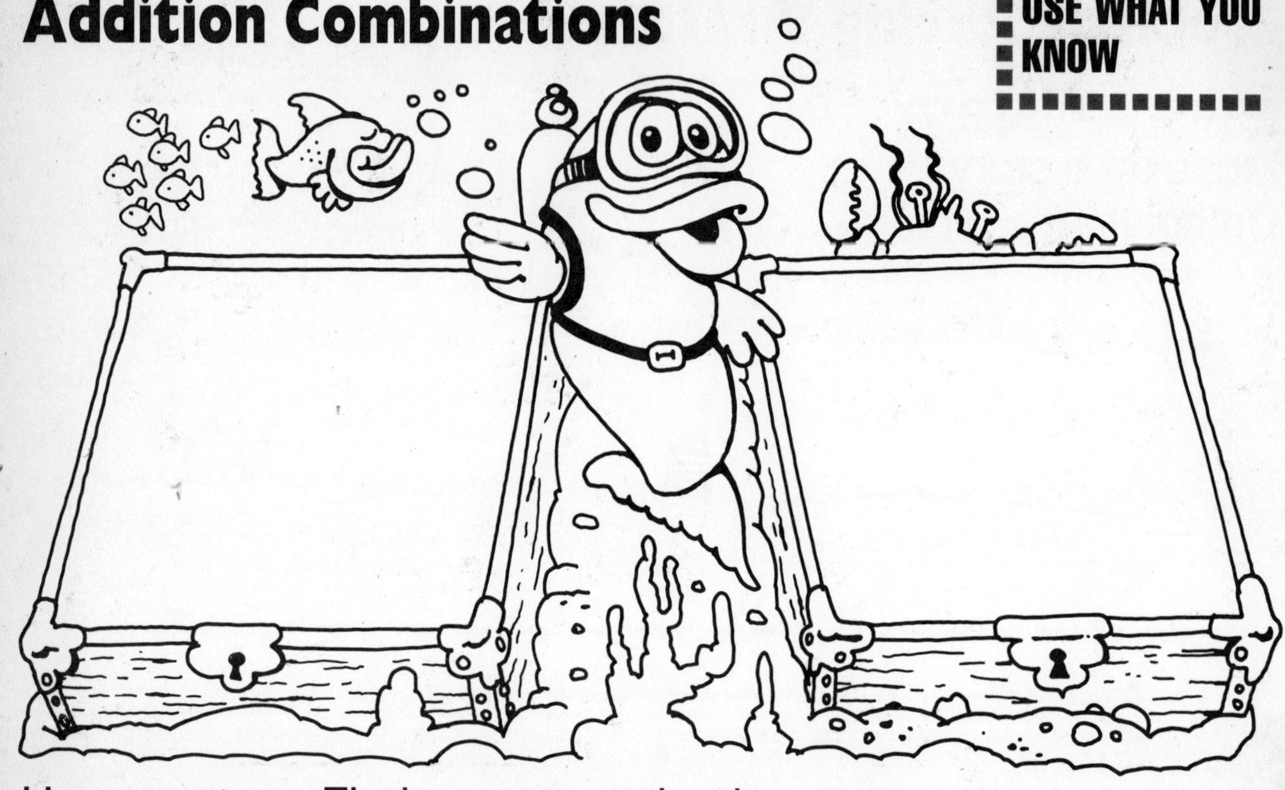

Use counters. Find ways to make the sums.
Then write the addition sentences.

1. 6 + 1 = 3
2. 3 + 2 = 3
3. 10 + 6 = 3
4. 4 + 5 = 3

---

5. 1 + 3 = 4
6. 4 + 2 = 4
7. 6 + 9 = 4
8. 3 + 5 = 4
9. 3 + 8 = 4

Number Sense

10. Ring the sum that is less.

5 + 2 = ____ 5 + 0 = ____

Use with text pages 53–54.

Name ________________________________

2.7
USE WHAT YOU KNOW

More Addition Combinations

Put in (paper clip).

Find ways to make the sums.

1. 4 + 2 = 5
2. 5 + 5 = 5
3. 3 + 2 = 5
4. 6 + 2 = 5
5. 1 + 5 = 5
6. 3 + 4 = 5

---

7. 3 + 4 = 6
8. 3 + 1 = 6
9. 5 + 6 = 6
10. 2 + 3 = 6
11. 8 + 10 = 6
12. 5 + 5 = 6
13. 1 + 3 = 6

Reasoning

14. Do both groups have the same number?
Ring **Yes** or **No**. Yes No

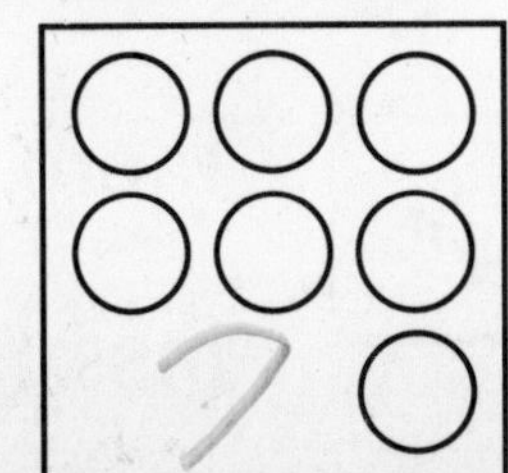

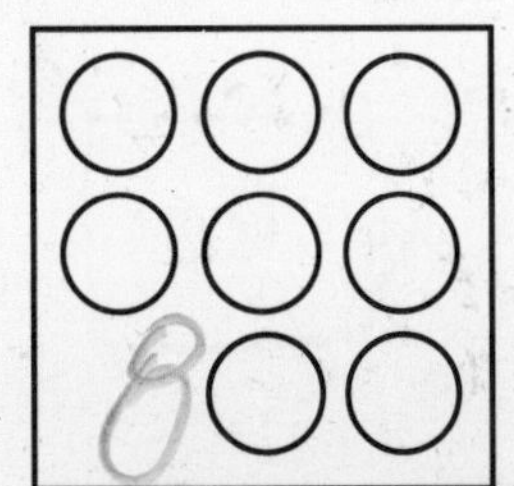

Name ____________________

2.8 USE WHAT YOU KNOW

Vertical Addition

Complete.

1\.

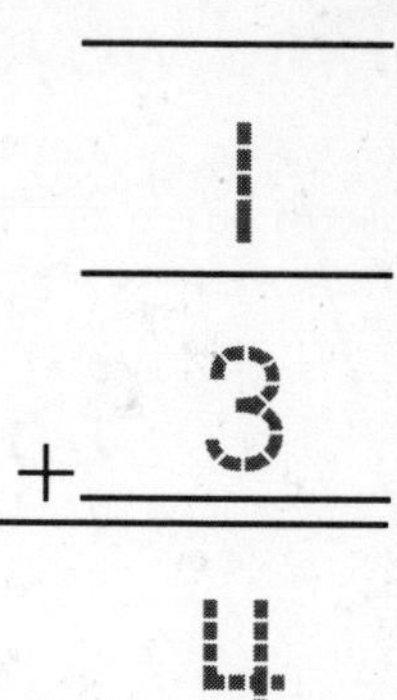

1 + 3 = 4

2\.

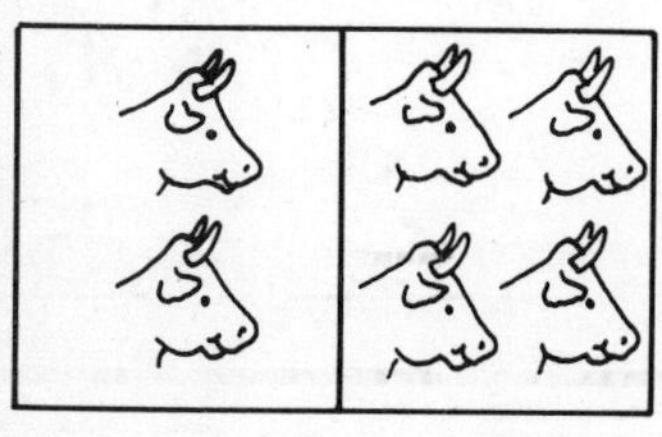

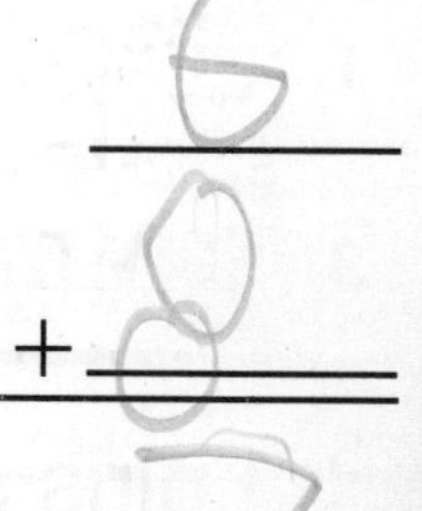

___ + ___ = ___

3\.

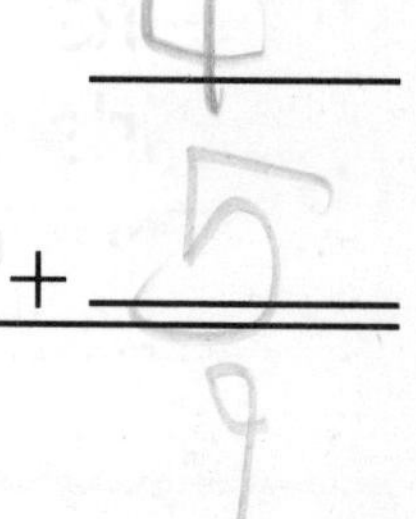

___ + ___ = ___

Number Sense

4\. What is the total cost? Ring the better estimate.

and

more than 5¢

less than 5¢

Use with text pages 57–58.

Name ______________________________

2.9
USE WHAT YOU KNOW

Problem-Solving Strategy

Act It Out

Read the story. Act it out.
Write the number sentence.

1. 3 girls walk.
   2 girls run.
   How many girls are there? 3 + 2 = 5

2. 4 girls smile.
   1 girl frowns.
   How many girls are there? ____ + ____ = ____

3. 5 girls play.
   0 girls work.
   How many girls are there? ____ + ____ = ____

4. 2 boys jump.
   2 boys hop.
   How many boys are there? ____ + ____ = ____

Visual Thinking

5. Ring the ones that have the same sum.

▲▲+▲▲▲▲ ▲+▲▲▲

Name ______________________________

Understanding Subtraction

Tell a story to a friend. Write how many.

How many?	How many go away?	How many are left?

1.

3 ____ 1 ____ 2 ____

2.

____ ____ ____

3.

____ ____ ____

Story Corner

4. Look at the picture.
Write the missing numbers.

I see ______ boys.

I see ______ boy run away.

I see ______ boys left.

Use with text pages 69–70.

Name ____________________

3.2
USE WHAT YOU KNOW

Subtraction Sentences

Write each subtraction sentence.

1\.

4 – 2 = 2

2\.

3 – 5 = 1

3\.

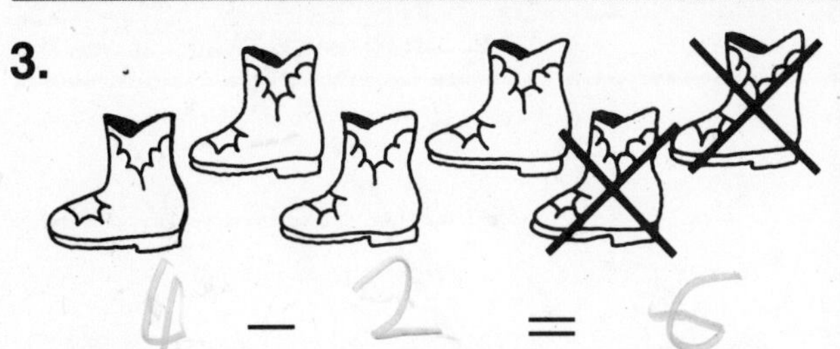

4 – 2 = 6

4\.

2 – 1 = 3

5\.

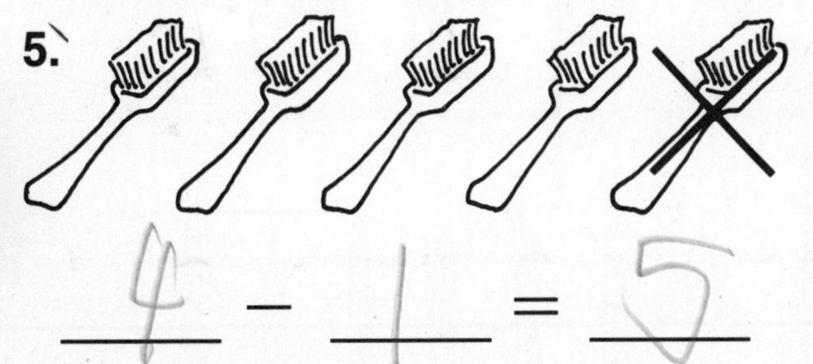

4 – 1 = 5

6\.

1 – 1 = 2

Number Sense

Write each number.

7\. How many faces? 1

How many ☺? 3

How many ☹? 6

8\. How many faces? 8

How many ☺? 10

How many ☹? 9

Use with text pages 71–72.

Name ______________________________

3.3
USE WHAT YOU KNOW

Zero Property

Write how many are left.

1.

2 − 0 = 2

2.

3 − 3 = ____

3.

6 − 6 = ____

4.

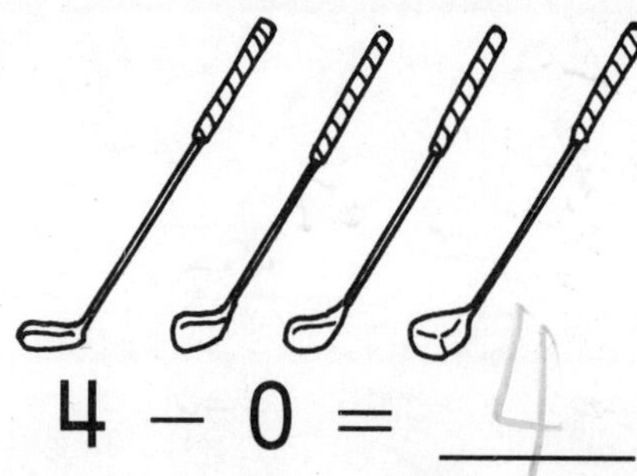

4 − 0 = ____

5.

5 − 0 = ____

6.

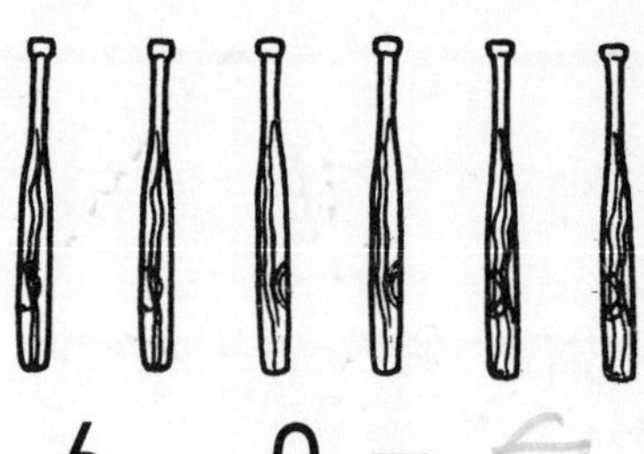

6 − 0 = ____

7.

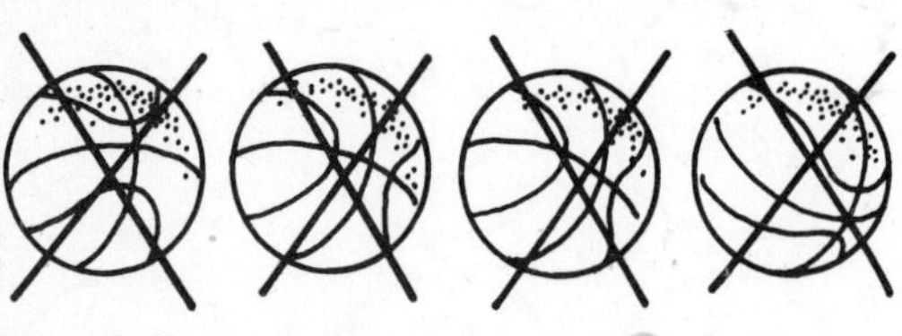

4 − 4 = ____

8.

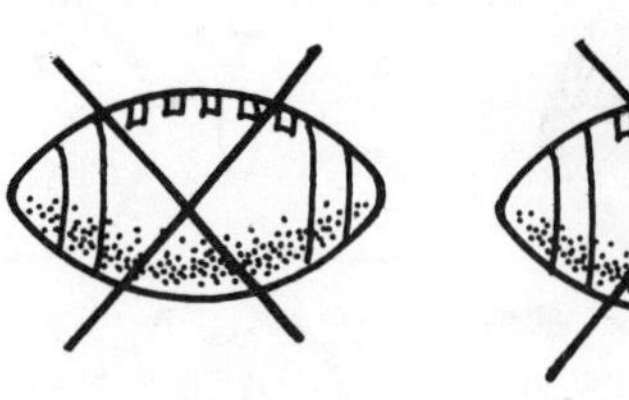

2 − 2 = ____

Reasoning

9. You pick 3  .
You eat all but 1.
How many do you eat? ____ apples

Name ____________________

3.4
USE WHAT YOU KNOW

More Subtraction Sentences

Cross out. Then write how many are left.

1.
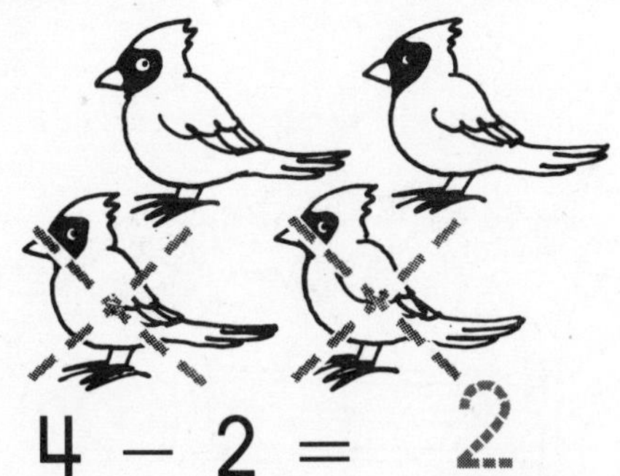

$4 - 2 =$ 2

2.

$6 - 1 =$ 7

3.
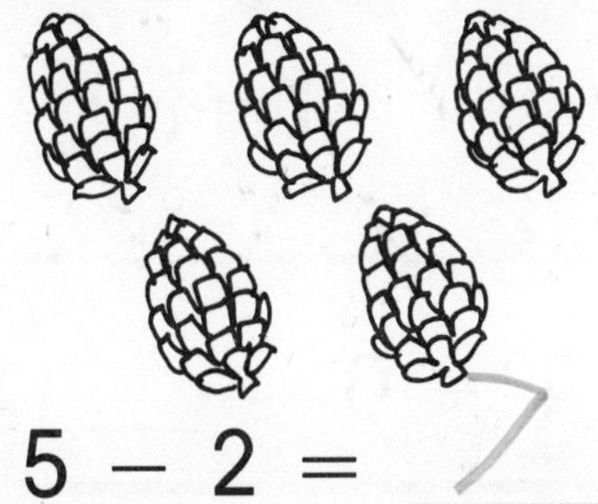

$5 - 2 =$ 7

4.

$4 - 1 =$ 5

5.
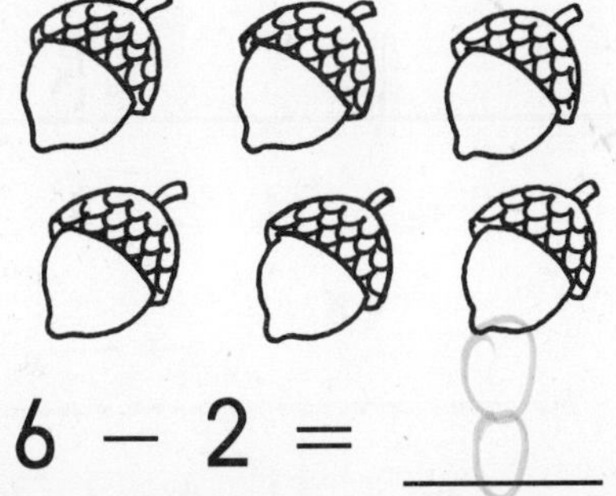

$6 - 2 =$ 8

6.

$5 - 0 =$ 5

Story Corner

7. Tell a story to a friend.
Write the subtraction sentence.

3 – 3 = 3

Name ______________________________

3.5
USE WHAT YOU KNOW

Problem Solving

Choose the Operation

Tell a story to answer each question.
Ring **Add** or **Subtract**.

1. 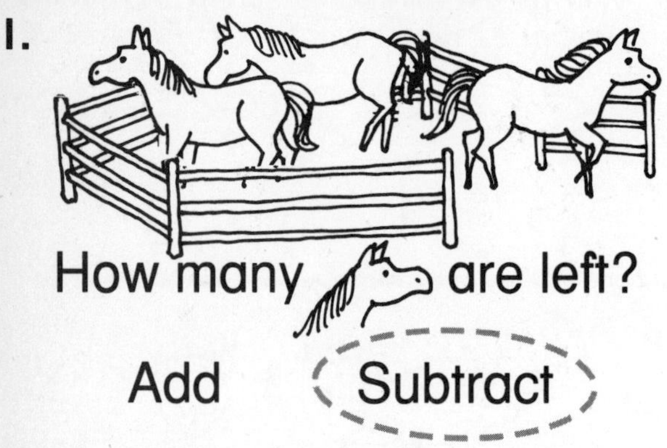

How many [horse] are left?

Add   (Subtract)

2. 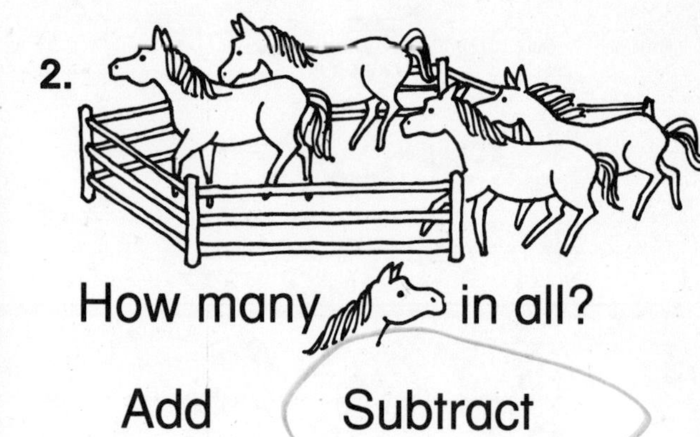

How many [horse] in all?

Add   Subtract

Match each number sentence.

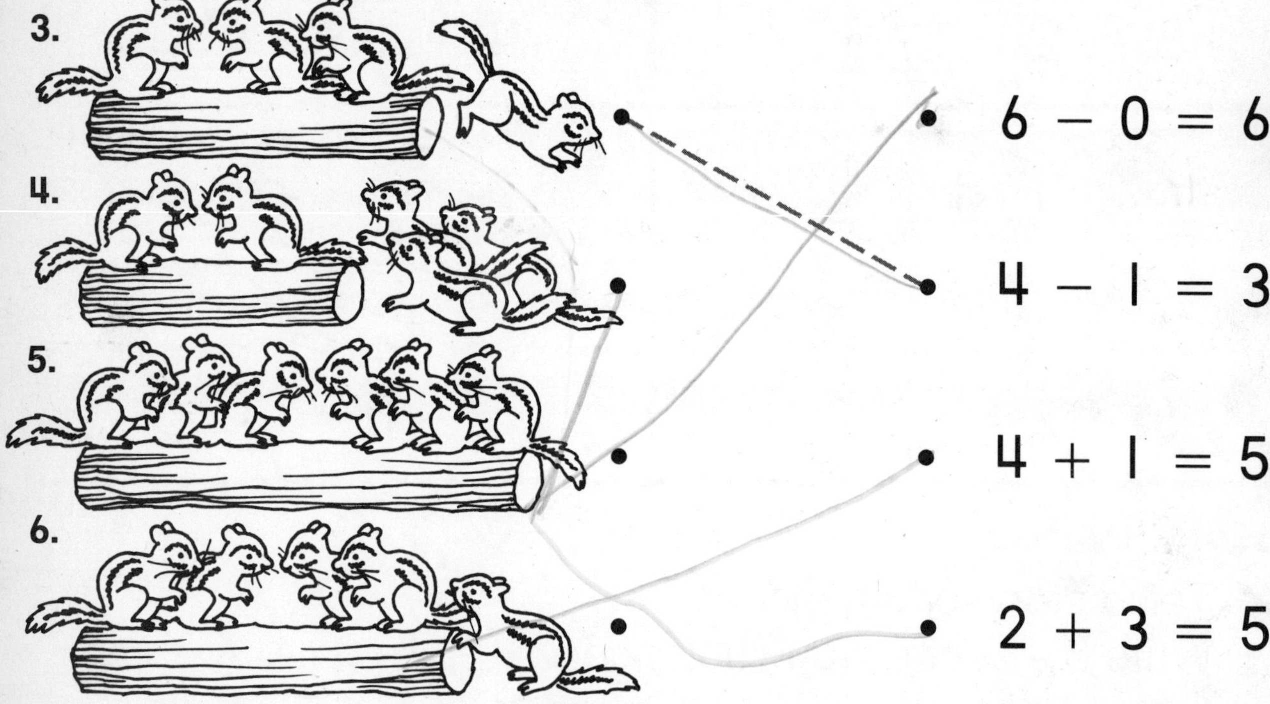

3.
4.
5.
6.

6 − 0 = 6

4 − 1 = 3

4 + 1 = 5

2 + 3 = 5

Reasoning

7. Write the missing sign.

3 ◯ 3 = 6   3 ◯ 3 = 0   0 ◯ 3 = 3

Use with text pages 77–78.

Name ______________________

3.6 USE WHAT YOU KNOW

Subtraction Combinations

Put in 4  .

Find ways to subtract from 4.

1. 4 − 2 = 2
2. 4 − ____ = ____
3. 4 − ____ = ____
4. 4 − ____ = ____
5. 4 − ____ = ____

Subtract.

6.	3 − 1 = ___	5 − 0 = ___	4 − 4 = ___
7.	6 − 6 = ___	2 − 1 = ___	1 − 0 = ___
8.	4 − 3 = ___	3 − 2 = ___	6 − 4 = ___
9.	2 − 2 = ___	5 − 2 = ___	6 − 1 = ___
10.	3 − 0 = ___	6 − 3 = ___	1 − 1 = ___

Number Sense

Ring the better estimate.

11. 9 − 3 = ? more than 9 less than 9

Name ____________________

3.7 USE WHAT YOU KNOW

More Subtraction Combinations

Put in 5  .

Find ways to subtract from 5.

1. 5 − 5 = 0
2. 5 − ____ = ____
3. 5 − ____ = ____
4. 5 − ____ = ____
5. 5 − ____ = ____
6. 5 − ____ = ____

Look for a pattern. Subtract.

7. 6 − 3 = ___ 6 − 2 = ___ 6 − 1 = ___
8. 5 − 2 = ___ 5 − 1 = ___ 5 − 0 = ___
9. 5 − 1 = ___ 5 − 2 = ___ 5 − 3 = ___
10. 4 − 0 = ___ 4 − 1 = ___ 4 − 2 = ___

Number Sense

11. Which answer will be the least? Ring it. Then solve to check.

10 − 3 = ___ 10 − 2 = ___ 10 − 1 = ___

Use with text pages 83–84.

Name ______________________________

3.8 USE WHAT YOU KNOW

Vertical Subtraction

Subtract.

1.  

$$\begin{array}{r} 4 \\ -2 \\ \hline 2 \end{array}$$

2.  

$$\begin{array}{r} 5 \\ -1 \\ \hline \end{array}$$

3. 

$$\begin{array}{r} 6 \\ -0 \\ \hline \end{array}$$

4. 

$$\begin{array}{r} 4 \\ -3 \\ \hline \end{array}$$

5. 

$$\begin{array}{r} 5¢ \\ -5¢ \\ \hline ¢ \end{array}$$

6. 

$$\begin{array}{r} 6¢ \\ -1¢ \\ \hline ¢ \end{array}$$

7.    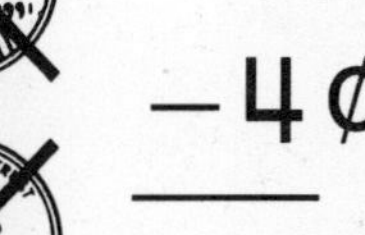

$$\begin{array}{r} 6¢ \\ -4¢ \\ \hline ¢ \end{array}$$

8.    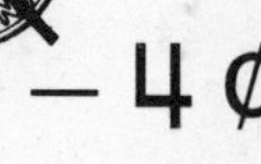

$$\begin{array}{r} 5¢ \\ -4¢ \\ \hline ¢ \end{array}$$

Visual Thinking

9. Draw dots to continue the pattern.

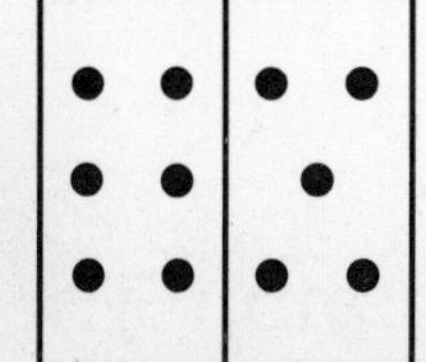 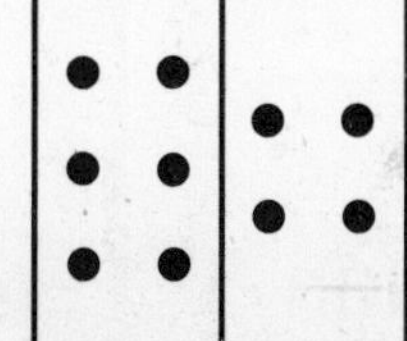 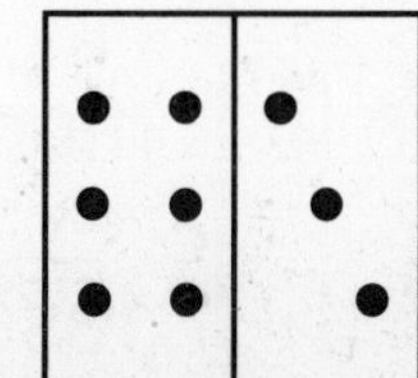 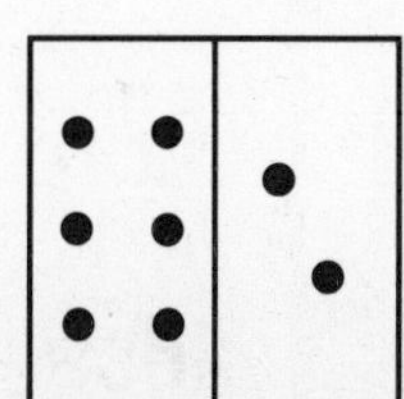 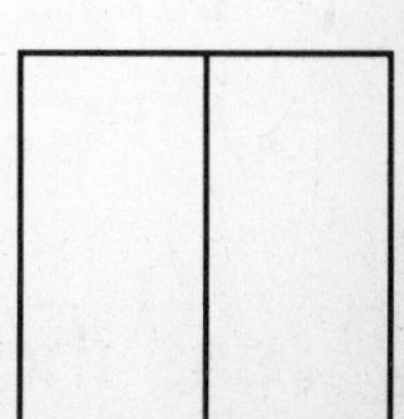

Name ____________________

Addition and Subtraction

Add or subtract.

1.

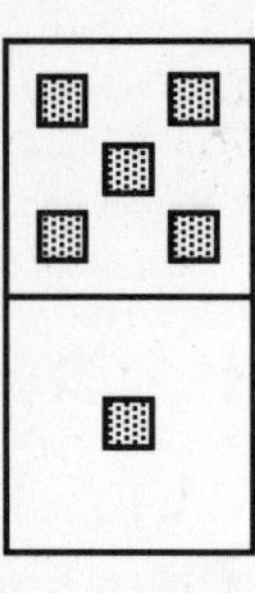

$$\begin{array}{r} 5 \\ +1 \\ \hline 6 \end{array}$$

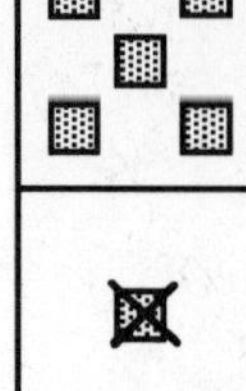

$$\begin{array}{r} 6 \\ -1 \\ \hline \end{array}$$

$$\begin{array}{r} 6 \\ -5 \\ \hline \end{array}$$

2.

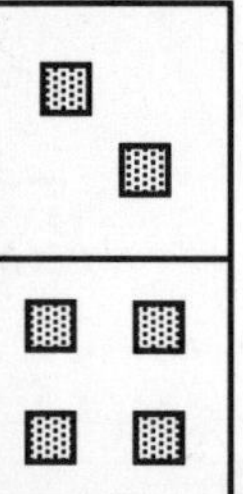

$$\begin{array}{r} 2 \\ +4 \\ \hline \end{array}$$

$$\begin{array}{r} 6 \\ -4 \\ \hline \end{array}$$

$$\begin{array}{r} 6 \\ -2 \\ \hline \end{array}$$

3.

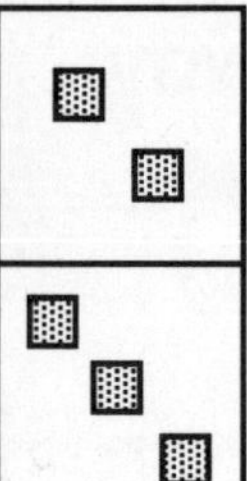

$$\begin{array}{r} 2 \\ +3 \\ \hline \end{array}$$

$$\begin{array}{r} 5 \\ -3 \\ \hline \end{array}$$

$$\begin{array}{r} 5 \\ -2 \\ \hline \end{array}$$

Number Sense

4. Ring the better estimate.

$\begin{array}{r} 4 \\ +1 \\ \hline ? \end{array}$	$\begin{array}{r} 4 \\ -1 \\ \hline ? \end{array}$	$\begin{array}{r} 3 \\ +2 \\ \hline ? \end{array}$	$\begin{array}{r} 3 \\ -2 \\ \hline ? \end{array}$
more than 4	more than 4	more than 3	more than 3
less than 4	less than 4	less than 3	less than 3

Use with text pages 87–88.

Name ____________________

3.10
USE WHAT YOU KNOW

Problem Solving

Choose the Question

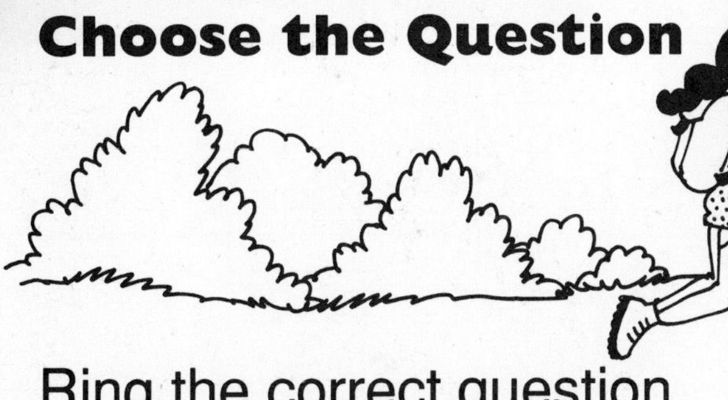

Ring the correct question.

1. Rosa sees 3 .
   Then all of them fly away.

   How many in all?

   How many are left?

2. Chad counts 5 .
   Then he sees 1 more.

   How many in all?

   How many are left?

3. Mrs. Davis finds 2 .
   Then she finds 2 more.

   How many in all?

   How many are left?

4. Mr. Davis sees 2 .
   Then 1 hops away.

   How many in all?

   How many are left?

5. Chad watches 4 .
   Then 3 run away.

   How many in all?

   How many are left?

6. Rosa counts 3 .
   Then she counts 3 more.

   How many in all?

   How many are left?

Story Corner

7. Tell a story about the picture.
   Write the number sentence.

____ ◯ ____ = ____

Name ____________________

4.1
USE WHAT YOU KNOW

Counting On

Count on to add. Write each sum.

1.

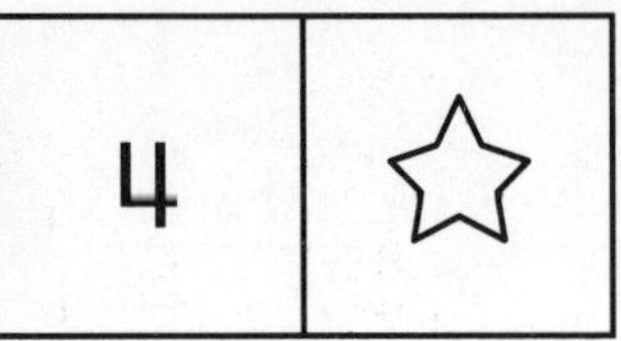

4 + 1 = 5

4	☆☆

4 + 2 = ____

2.

8	☆

8 + 1 = ____

5	☆☆

5 + 2 = ____

3.

5	☆

5 + 1 = ____

2	☆☆

2 + 2 = ____

4.

6 + 1 = ____ 7 + 1 = ____ 8 + 1 = ____

5.

8 + 2 = ____ 7 + 2 = ____ 6 + 2 = ____

Number Sense

6. Ring the one that has the greatest sum.

10 + 2 10 + 1 10 + 0

Use with text pages 101–102.

Name ______________________________

More Counting On

Count on to add. Write each sum.

1. 

3	5	1	8
+ 2	+ 2	+ 2	+ 2
5			

2.

2	5	8	1	9	7
+ 1	+ 1	+ 1	+ 1	+ 1	+ 1

3.

3	7	5	1	4	6
+ 3	+ 3	+ 3	+ 3	+ 3	+ 3

4.

7	5	9	8	6	6
+ 2	+ 3	+ 1	+ 2	+ 3	+ 2

5.

4	4	8	7	5	5
+ 3	+ 2	+ 1	+ 3	+ 2	+ 1

Number Sense

6. Ring the one that has the least sum.

9 + 2 9 + 1 9 + 3

Name ____________________

4.3 USE WHAT YOU KNOW

Counting On 1, 2, and 3

Count on to add. Write each sum.

1. 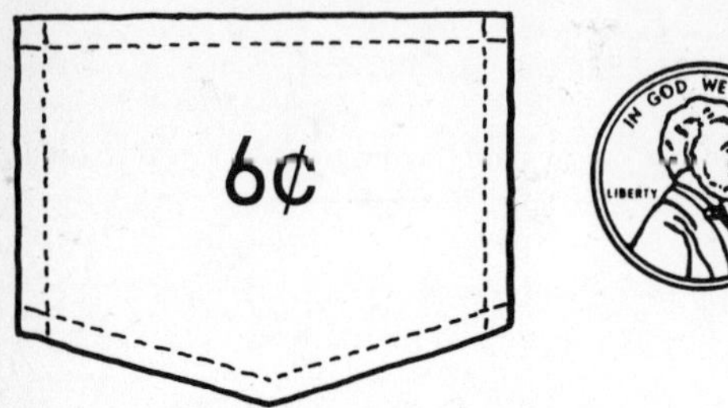

6¢ + 1¢ = 7 ¢

2. 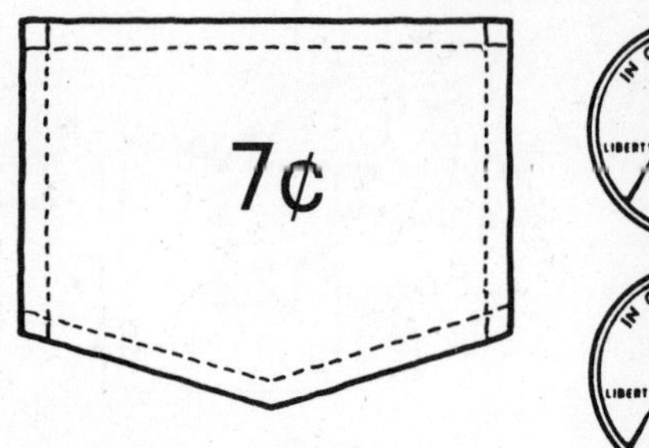

7¢ + 2¢ = ____ ¢

3. 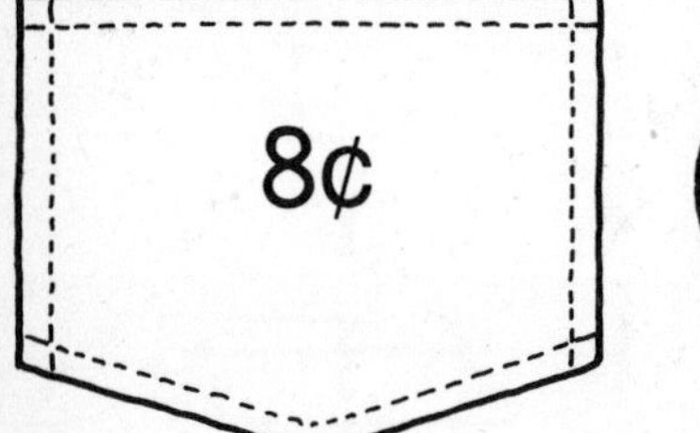

8¢ + 1¢ = ____ ¢

4. 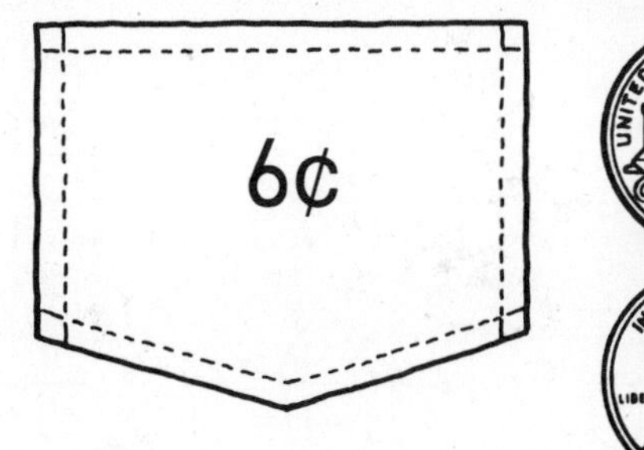

6¢ + 2¢ = ____ ¢

5. 

4¢ + 3¢ = ____ ¢

6. 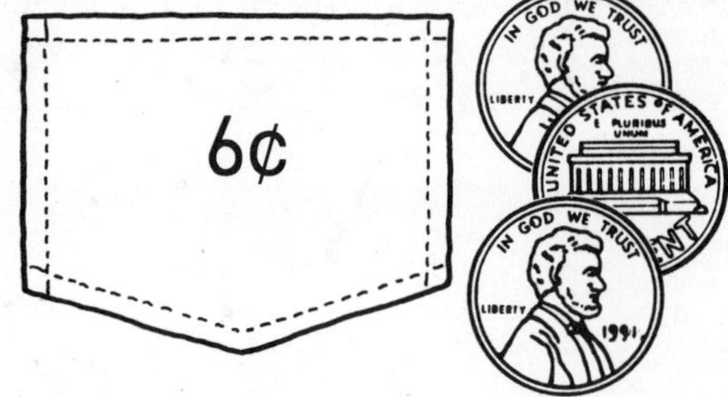

6¢ + 3¢ = ____ ¢

Reasoning

Solve.

7. Lee has 5¢.
Kara has 3¢ more than Lee.
Tom has 2¢ more than Kara.
How much money does Tom have? ____ ¢

Use with text pages 105–106.

Name ______________________________

4.4
USE WHAT YOU KNOW

Problem Solving

Use a Picture

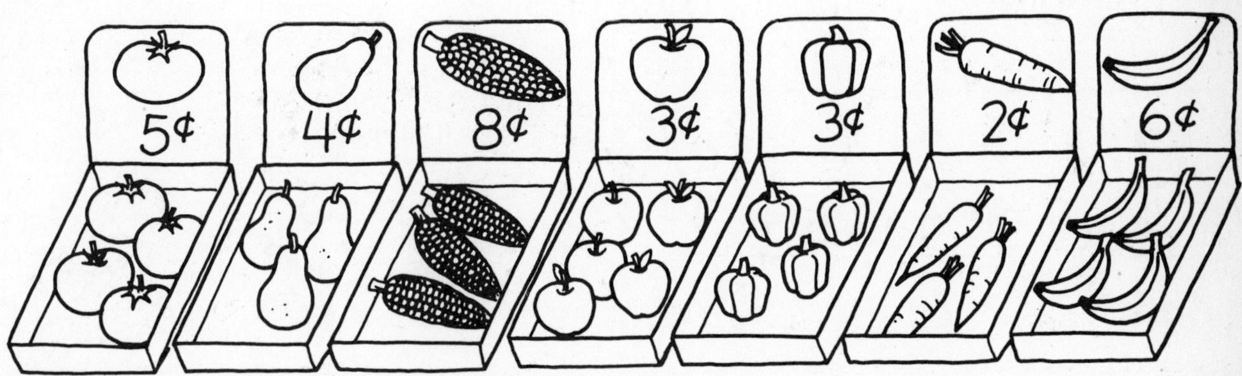

Write the addition fact to find the total amount.

1.

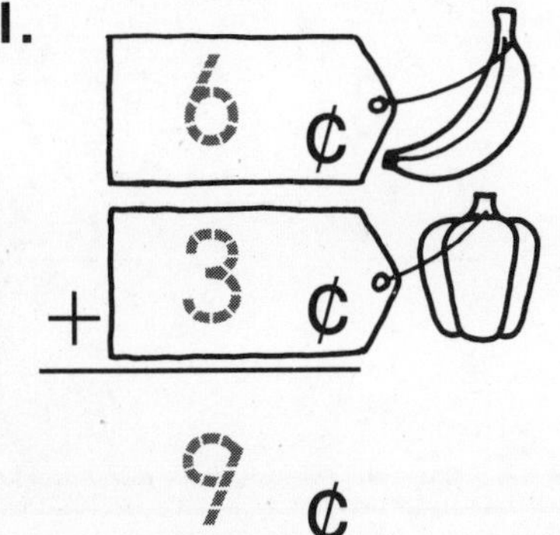

¢
+ ¢
______ ¢

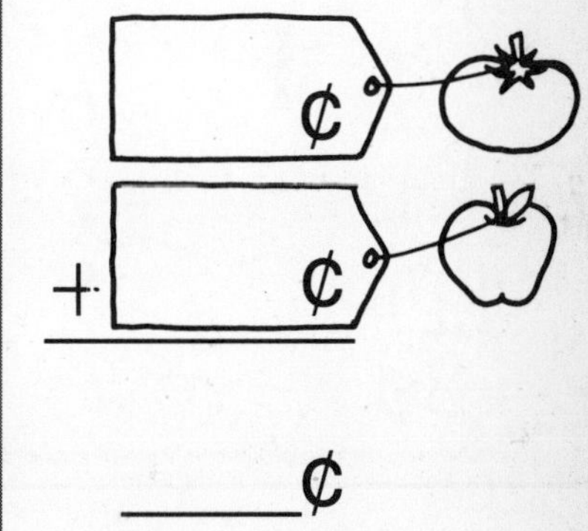

2.

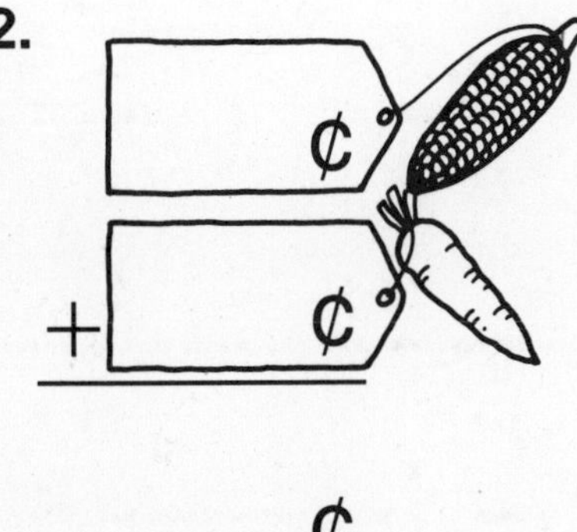

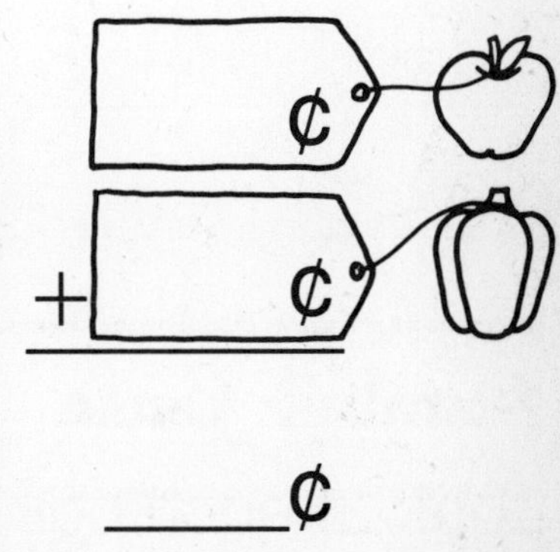

Story Corner

3. Look at the picture.
Make up a story problem.
Tell it to a friend.
Have a friend solve it.

Name ______________________________

4.5

USE WHAT YOU KNOW

Counting On

Mental Math

Ring the greater number. Then add.

(7) 8	2	(6) 7,8,9
+ 1	+ (6) 7,8	+ 3
8	8	9

1.

(9)	6	2	4	3	7
+ 1	+ 2	+ 3	+ 2	+ 4	+ 2
10					

2.

4	2	5	1	5	7
+ 1	+ 8	+ 3	+ 4	+ 1	+ 3

Number Sense

Look at each pair. Ring the numbers that have the sum that is less. Solve to check.

3.

1	8
+ 8	+ 2

4.

3	2
+ 5	+ 5

5.

4	4
+ 3	+ 2

Use with text pages 111–112.

Name ______________________________

4.6 USE WHAT YOU KNOW

Doubles

Complete each doubles fact.
Write each sum.

1. 4 + <u>4</u> = <u>8</u> | 1 + ____ = ____

2. 0 + ____ = ____ | 5 + ____ = ____

3. 3 + 3 | 1 + 1 | 4 + 4 | 2 + 2 | 0 + 0 | 5 + 5

Write each sum. Ring each double.

4. 2 + 6 | 7 + 1 | 3 + 3 | 0 + 0 | 6 + 3 | 5 + 5

5. 4 + 4 | 3 + 7 | 5 + 3 | 2 + 2 | 2 + 5 | 1 + 1

Reasoning

Solve.

6. Chen has 3¢.
Jon has double this amount.
Mary has 1¢ more than Jon.
How much money
does Mary have? ______¢

Name ______________________________

4.7 USE WHAT YOU KNOW

Addition Table

Write the missing sums.

+	0	1	2	3	4	5	6	7	8
0	0	1	2		4	5		7	
1	1	2	3			6		8	9
2	2		4	5	6	7	8		10
3	3				7		9	10	
4	4	5	6		8	9			
5	5		7	8		10			
6	6	7		9					
7	7		9						
8	8		10						

Reasoning

Peter saw 3 red and 5 brown birds.
Jane saw 4 red and 4 brown birds.
Enrico saw 2 red and 7 brown birds.
Which children saw the same number of birds?

______________ and ______________

Name ______________________________

4.8
USE WHAT YOU KNOW

Adding Three Numbers

Add. Start with the ringed numbers.

1. ③ + ③ + 4 | 3 + ③ + ④

6 + 4 = 10 | 3 + 7 = 10

2. ② + ⑤ + 1 | 2 + ⑤ + ①

___ + ___ = ___ | ___ + ___ = ___

Add.

3.

1	4	3	6	1	1
1	2	4	3	3	3
+ 8	+ 2	+ 1	+ 1	+ 5	+ 3

4.

4	1	2	3	1	6
4	2	3	2	7	4
+ 1	+ 7	+ 4	+ 5	+ 1	+ 0

Reasoning

5. Use doubles to add.
Ring the numbers you would add first.

1 + 5 + 4

___ + ___ = ___

Use with text pages 117–118.

Name ____________________

4.9 USE WHAT YOU KNOW

Making Arrangements

Color 6 different  .

Use yellow 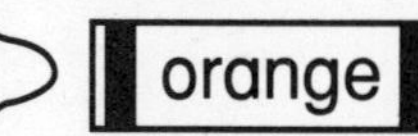

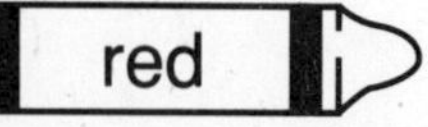

.

Each part of the ant must be a different color.

1\.

2\.

3\.

4\.

5\.

6\.

Visual Thinking

7\. Ring the two pictures that are the same.

    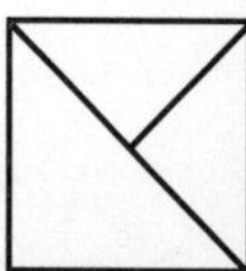

Use with text pages 119–120.

Name ________________________________

4.10 USE WHAT YOU KNOW

Problem Solving

Too Much Information

Draw a line through the sentence you do not need. Then solve.

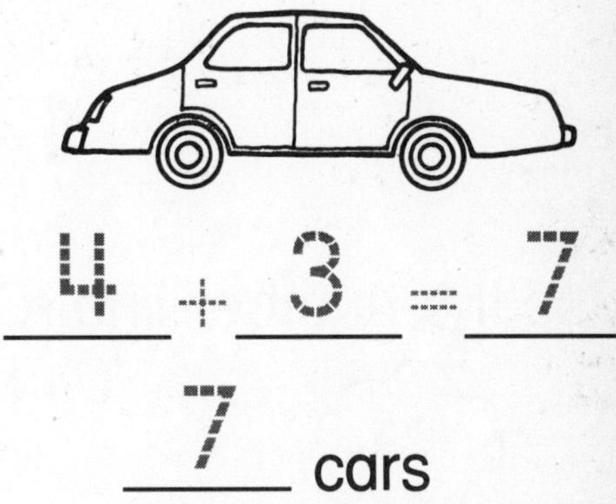

1. There are 4 cars on the road.
   ~~There are 2 trucks on the road.~~
   Then 3 more cars come.
   How many cars are there?

   4 + 3 = 7

   7 cars

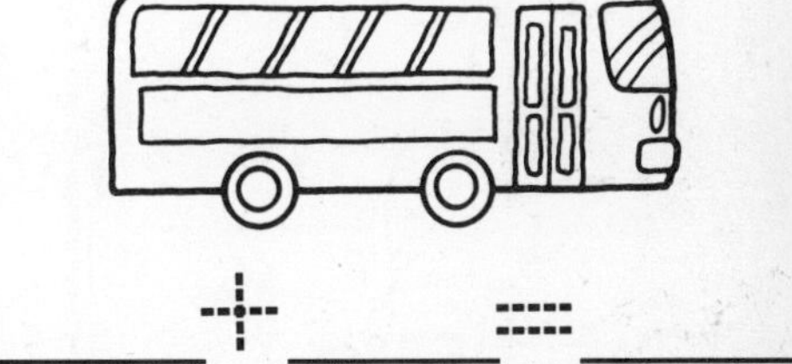

2. Mr. Ladd sees 4 buses.
   Then he sees 4 more buses.
   He sees 1 train, too.
   How many buses does he see?

   ____ + ____ = ____

   ____ buses

3. Anna counts 5 trees.
   She counts 3 stop signs.
   Then she counts 6 more stop signs. How many stop signs does she see?

   ____ + ____ = ____

   ____ stop signs

Story Corner

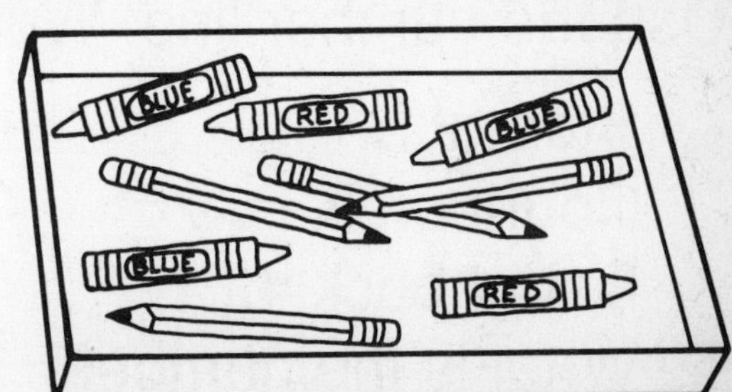

4. Look at the picture.
   Make up a story problem.
   Tell it to a friend.
   Have a friend solve it.

Name ______________________

5.1
USE WHAT YOU KNOW

Counting Back

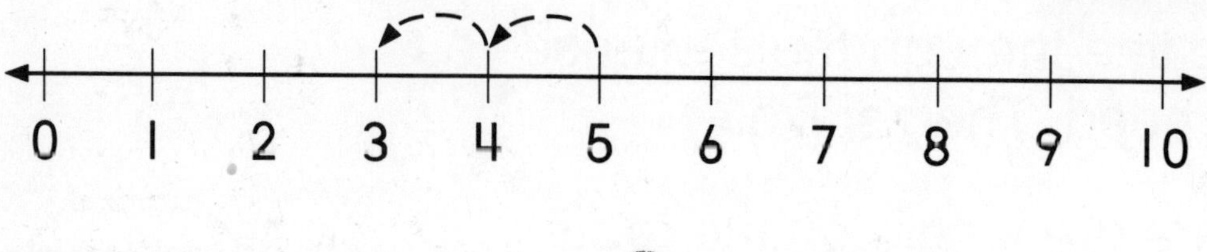

5 − 2 = 3

Use the number line. Count back to subtract.

3,2

6,5,4

1.	4 − 1 = 3	3 − 1 = ____	6 − 2 = ____
2.	6 − 1 = ____	5 − 2 = ____	8 − 1 = ____
3.	5 − 1 = ____	7 − 2 = ____	4 − 2 = ____
4.	9 − 2 = ____	3 − 2 = ____	10 − 1 = ____
5.	7 − 1 = ____	9 − 1 = ____	10 − 2 = ____

Number Sense

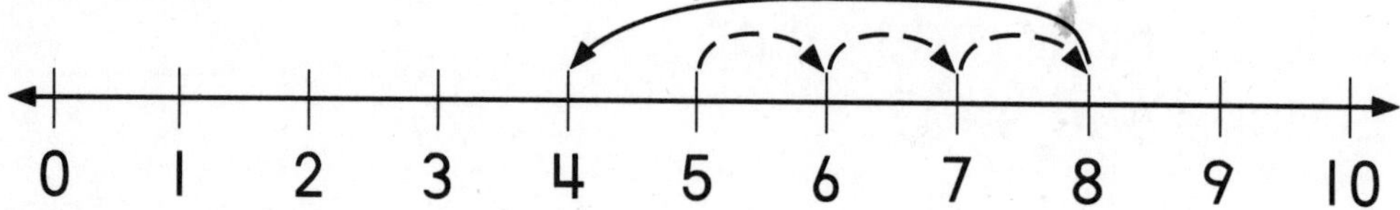

Use the number line. Write the number.

6. Start at 5.
   Count on 3.
   Count back 4.
   What is the number? ____

7. Start at 6.
   Count on 4.
   Count back 4.
   What is the number? ____

Use with text pages 131–132.

Name ____________________

5.2
USE WHAT YOU KNOW

More Counting Back

$9 - 1 = 8$ (9,8)	$7 - 2 = 5$ (7,6,5)	$6 - 2 = 4$ (6,5,4)

Count back to subtract.

1.

$8 - 1$	$10 - 1$	$4 - 1$	$5 - 1$	$3 - 1$	$6 - 1$

2.

$3 - 2$	$10 - 2$	$5 - 2$	$4 - 2$	$9 - 2$	$8 - 2$

3.

$7 - 1$	$9 - 2$	$9 - 1$	$6 - 2$	$5 - 1$	$7 - 2$

Reasoning

Solve.

4. Mario is 5 years old.
Sam is 2 years younger than Mario.
Fumi is 1 year younger than Sam.
How old is Fumi? ______ years old.

Use with text pages 133–134.

Name ______________________________

5.3 USE WHAT YOU KNOW

Counting Back 1, 2, and 3

Count back to subtract.
Use your answers from the box to color the picture blue.

1. 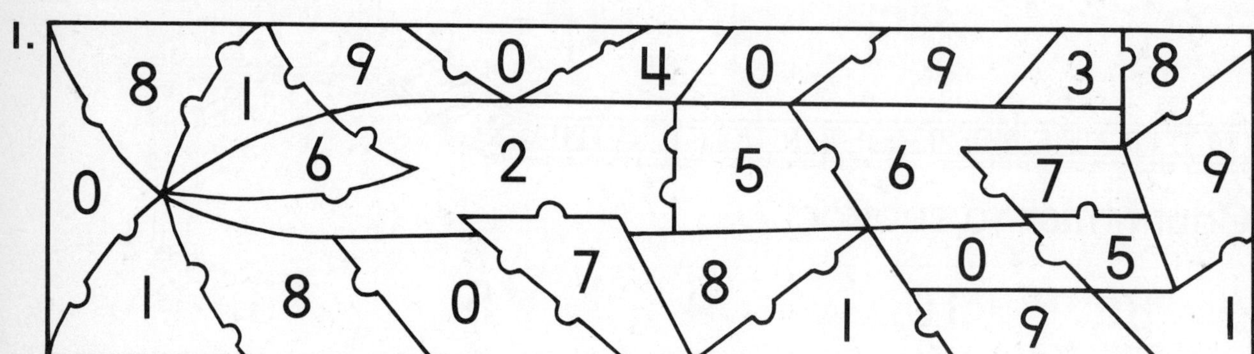

4 − 2 = 2	8 − 1 = ____	9 − 3 = ____
8 − 3 = ____	9 − 2 = ____	7 − 1 = ____
5 − 1 = ____	6 − 3 = ____	7 − 2 = ____

2. $\begin{array}{r} 8 \\ -2 \\ \hline \end{array}$ $\begin{array}{r} 5 \\ -3 \\ \hline \end{array}$ $\begin{array}{r} 3 \\ -1 \\ \hline \end{array}$ $\begin{array}{r} 6 \\ -2 \\ \hline \end{array}$ $\begin{array}{r} 9 \\ -1 \\ \hline \end{array}$ $\begin{array}{r} 7 \\ -3 \\ \hline \end{array}$

Number Sense

Look at each pair.
Ring the numbers that have the answer that is less. Solve to check.

3. $\begin{array}{r} 7 \\ -1 \\ \hline \end{array}$ $\begin{array}{r} 7 \\ -3 \\ \hline \end{array}$

4. $\begin{array}{r} 8 \\ -1 \\ \hline \end{array}$ $\begin{array}{r} 8 \\ -2 \\ \hline \end{array}$

5. $\begin{array}{r} 9 \\ -2 \\ \hline \end{array}$ $\begin{array}{r} 9 \\ -3 \\ \hline \end{array}$

Use with text pages 135–136.

Name ___________________________

5.4

USE WHAT YOU KNOW

Problem-Solving Strategy

Make a Model

You need counters and Workmat 1.
Use your counters to solve.

1. There are 8 .

   Then 3 go away.

   How many are left?

2. There are 5 .

   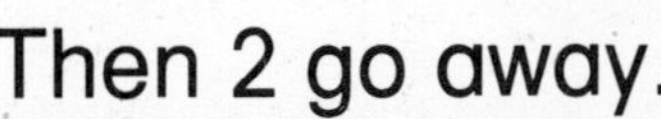

   Then 2 go away.

   How many are left?

   ______ 

3. There are 7 .

   Then 2 go away.

   How many are left?

   ______ 

4. There are 8 .

   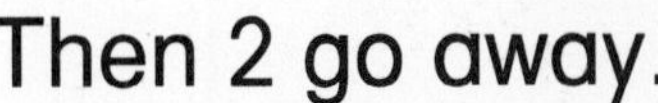

   Then 2 go away.

   How many are left?

   ______ 

5. There are 6 .

   There are 3 .

   How many more 

   than ?

   ______ more 

6. There are 9 .

   There are 3 .

   How many more 

   than ?

   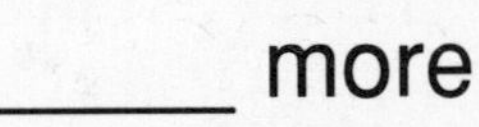

   ______ more 

Story Corner

7. Make up two story problems about a .
   Tell them to a friend. Have your friend solve each one.

Name ______________________

5.5 USE WHAT YOU KNOW

Subtracting Zero and Related Facts

Subtract. Write each difference.

1.	6	6	3	3	8	8
	− 1	− 5	− 0	− 3	− 3	− 5
	5	1				

2.	9	9	4	4	10	10
	− 2	− 7	− 1	− 3	− 3	− 7

3.	10	10	7	7	9	9
	− 2	− 8	− 2	− 5	− 3	− 6

4.	7	7	5	5	10	10
	− 3	− 4	− 3	− 2	− 1	− 9

Reasoning

Which boy is Terry? Ring him.

5. Jack has 3 balls.
Fred has 3 more balls than Jack.
Terry has more balls than Jack or Fred.

Use with text pages 141–142.

Name ______________________________

5.6 USE WHAT YOU KNOW

Addition and Subtraction

Write an addition fact. Cross out the black counters. Then write the subtraction fact.

1.

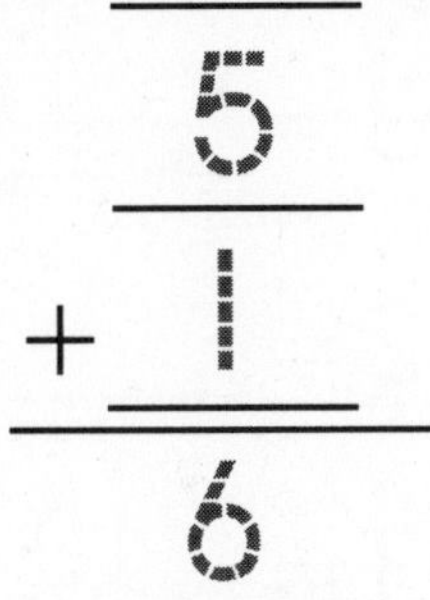

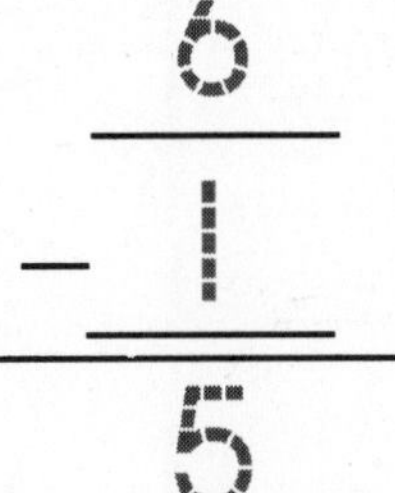

2. + ___ − ___

3. + ___ − ___

4. + ___ − ___

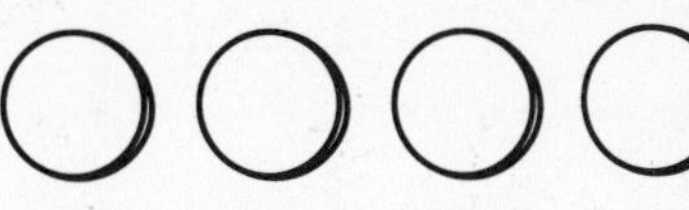

Visual Thinking

5. Think about the picture. Ring **Add** or **Subtract**.

Add Subtract

Use with text pages 143–144.

Name ______________________________

5.7
USE WHAT YOU KNOW

Fact Families

Use cubes. Add or subtract.
Write the numbers in each fact family.

1. 5 + 1 = 6	3 + 1 = ____	2 + 3 = ____
1 + 5 = 6	1 + 3 = ____	3 + 2 = ____
6 − 1 = 5	4 − 1 = ____	5 − 3 = ____
6 − 5 = 1	4 − 3 = ____	5 − 2 = ____
 5, 1, 6	____, ____, ____	____, ____, ____

Add or subtract.
Which sentence does not belong? Ring it.

2. 

2 + 6 = ____
6 + 2 = ____
8 − 2 = ____
7 − 2 = ____
8 − 6 = ____

3. 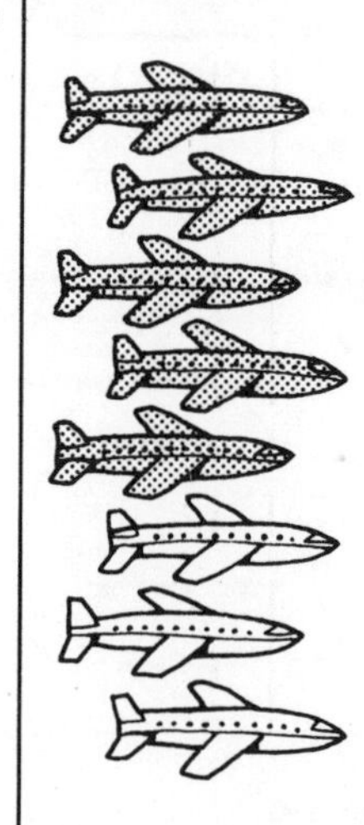

5 + 3 = ____
3 + 5 = ____
4 + 3 = ____
8 − 5 = ____
8 − 3 = ____

Problem Solving

Write the numbers.

4. Our sum is 5. Our difference is 1. ____ and ____

Use with text pages 145–146.

Name ____

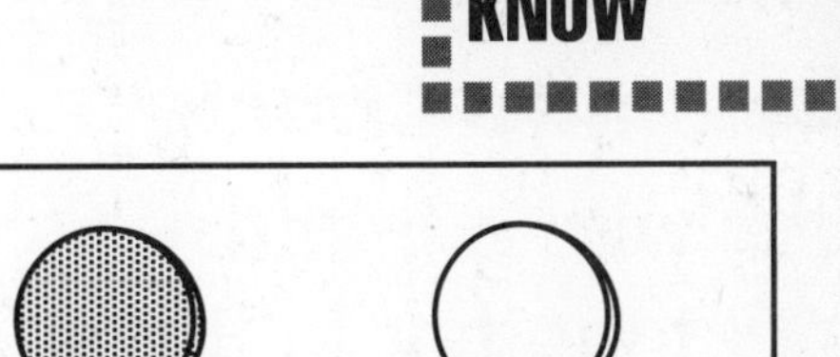

Exploring Probability

What can happen when you toss 3 two-color counters? Ring each group that shows what can happen.

red yellow

1.

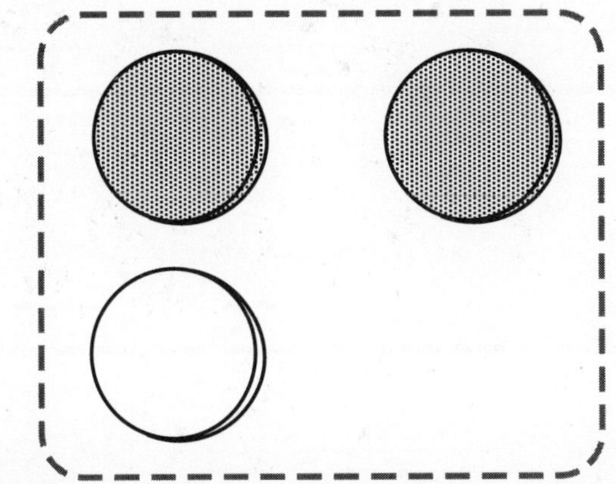

2.

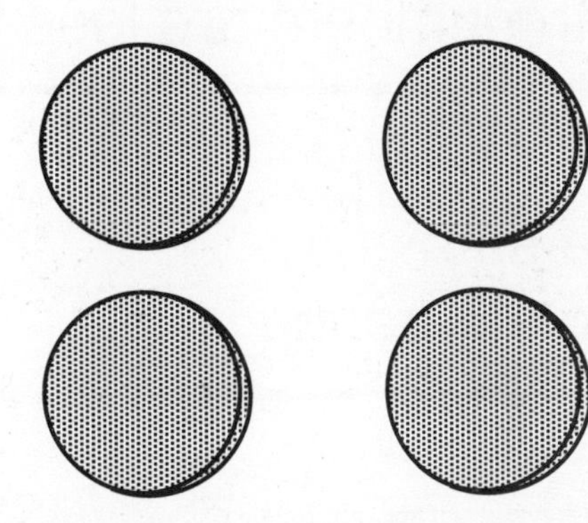

3.

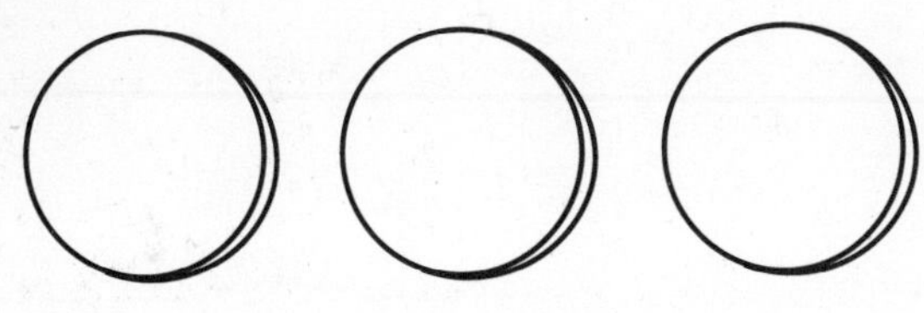

4.

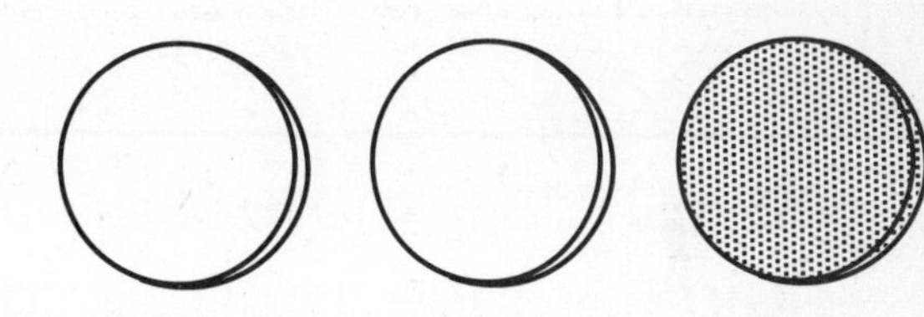

5.

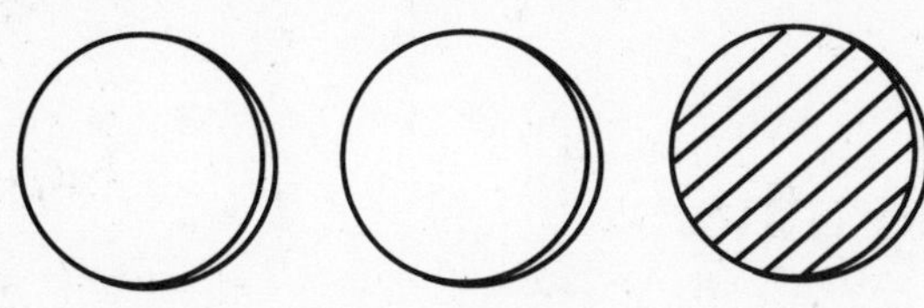

6.

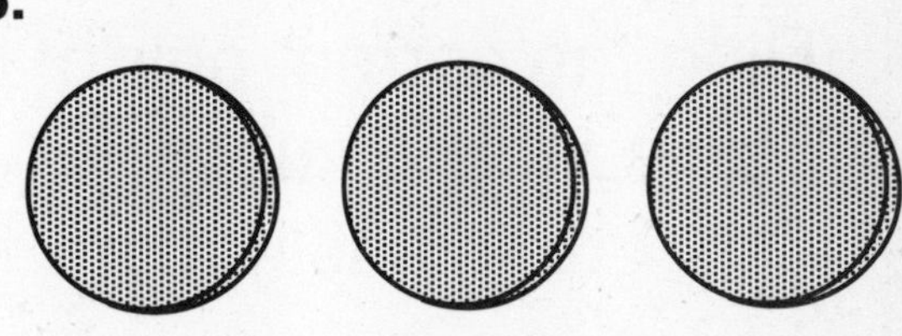

Problem Solving

7. Nick tossed 3 two-color counters.
He tossed them 2 times.
He got 4 red sides in all.
How many yellow sides in all did he get? _____ yellow

Name ____________________

5.9
USE WHAT YOU KNOW

Problem-Solving Strategy

Guess and Check

Work with a friend.
Work together to find the number pair.

1. The sum is 9.
   The difference is 1.
   Both numbers are less than 6. 5 and 4

2. The sum is 6.
   The difference is 0. ______ and ______

3. The sum is 2 more than 5.
   The difference is 1 less than 2. ______ and ______

4. The sum is 1 more than 7.
   The difference is 2 less than 4. ______ and ______

Visual Thinking

5. Ring the correct pair of cubes.
   The sum is 6 cubes.
   One group has 4 more than the other.

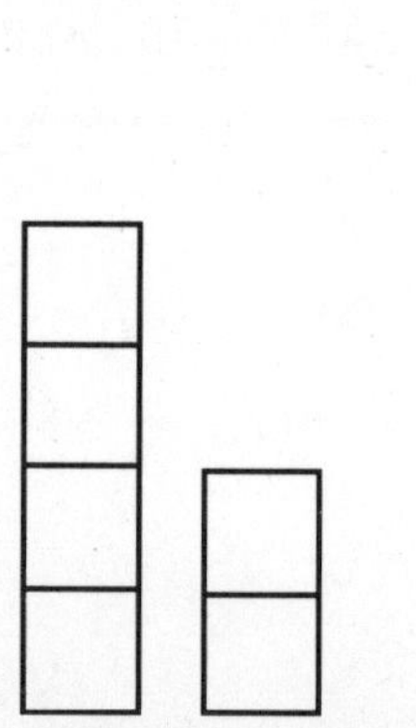
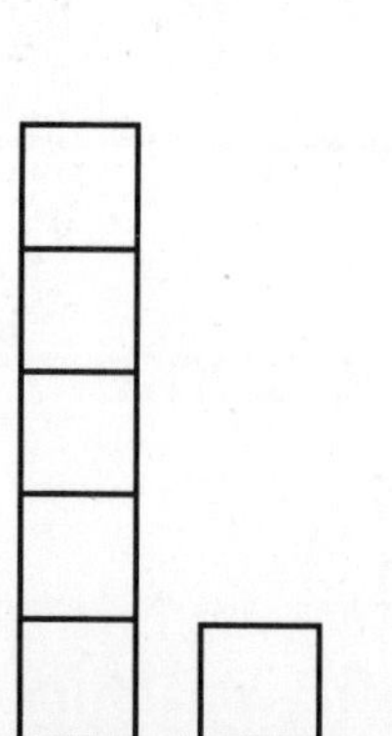
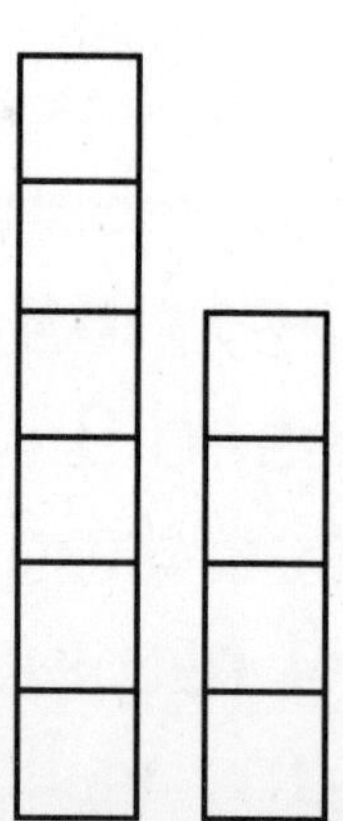

Use with text pages 149–150.

Name ___________________________

6.1 USE WHAT YOU KNOW

Solid Shapes

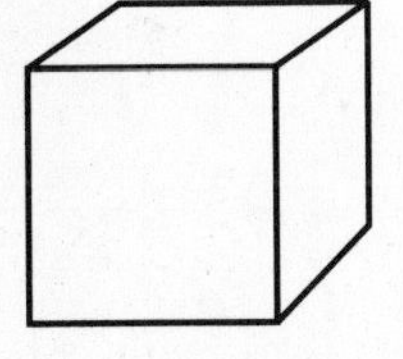
cube

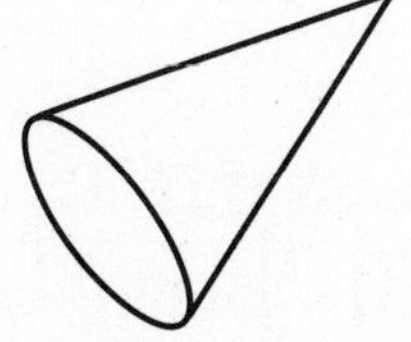
cone

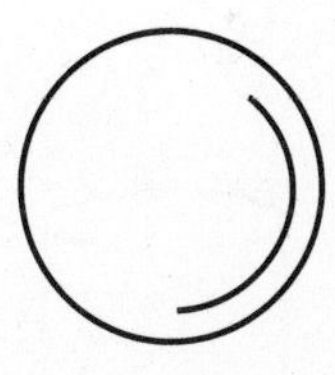
sphere

cylinder

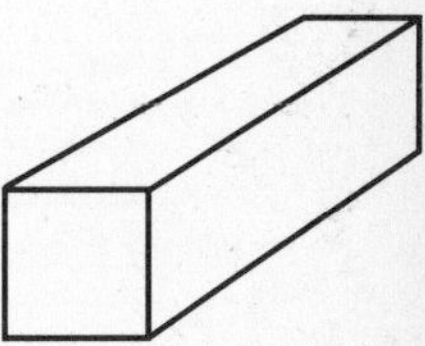
box

1. Color each cube shape red.
2. Color each sphere shape blue.
3. Ring each cylinder shape.
4. Draw an X on each cone shape.
5. Draw a line under each box shape.

Story Corner

6. Read this riddle.
   Ring the name of the shape.
   I am a solid shape.
   All my sides are flat.

cone cube sphere

Name ___________________________

6.2 USE WHAT YOU KNOW

More Solid Shapes

Use solid shapes.
Ring each shape that will stack.

1. 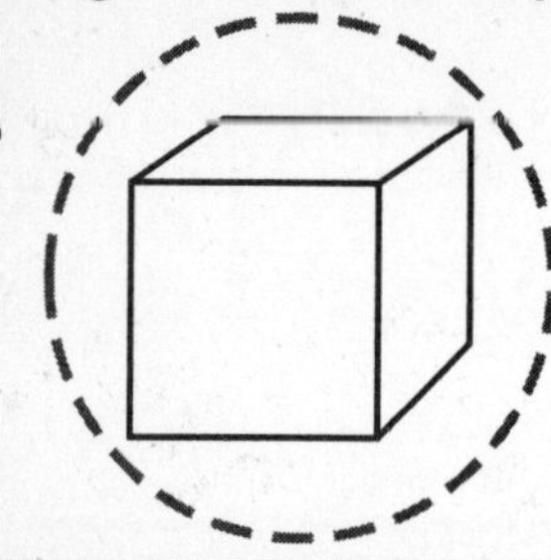 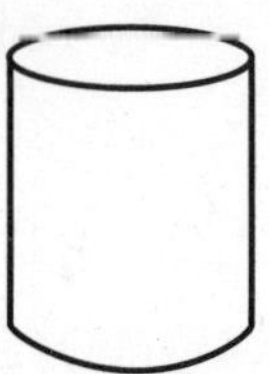 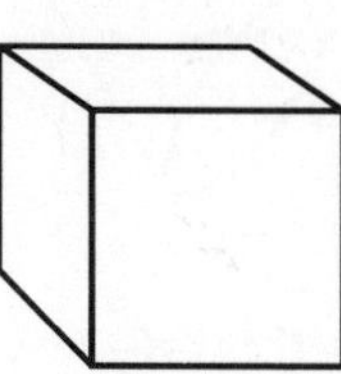 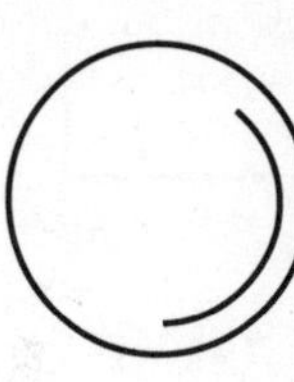

Draw an X on each shape that will roll.

2. 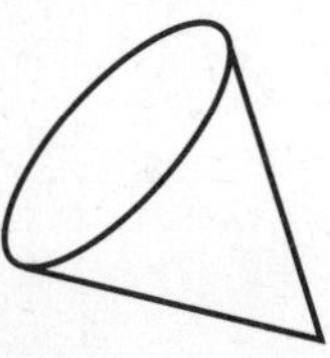 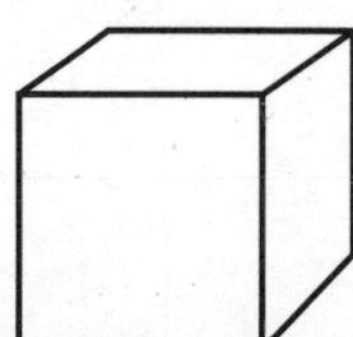 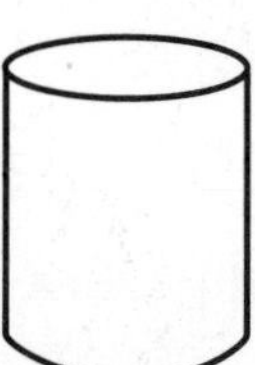 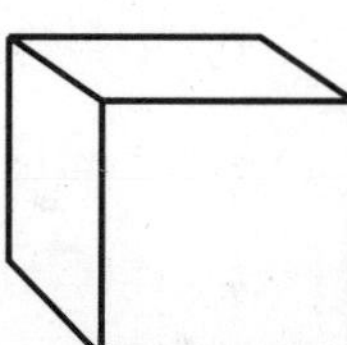 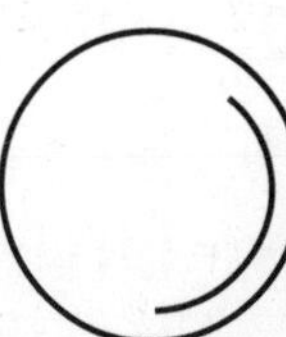

Color each shape that will slide.

3. 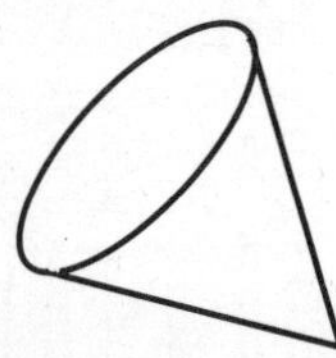 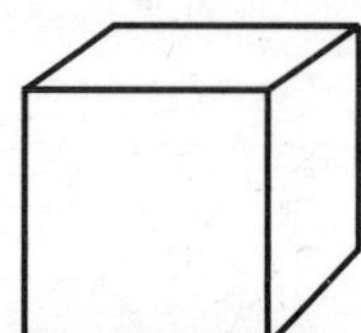 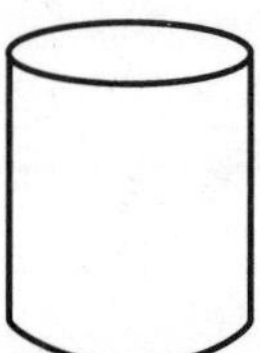 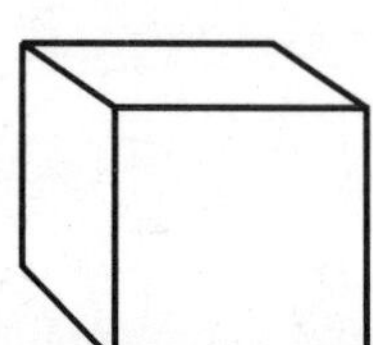 

Reasoning

Use solid shapes to build.
Ring the shape that must be on top.
Tell why.

4. 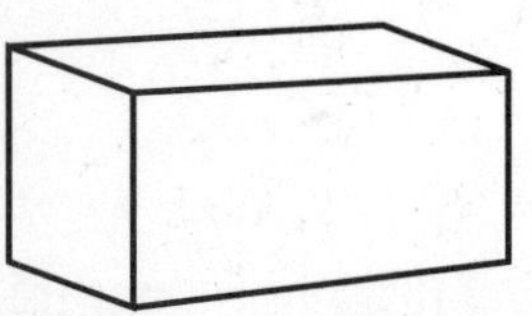 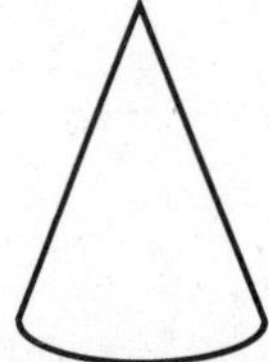  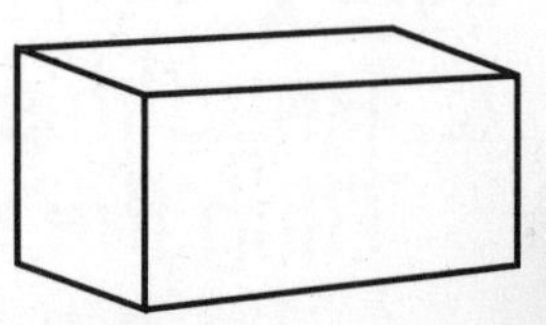

Use with text pages 161–162.

Name ____________________

6.3
USE WHAT YOU KNOW

Solid and Plane Shapes

Match the plane shape to the solid.

1.

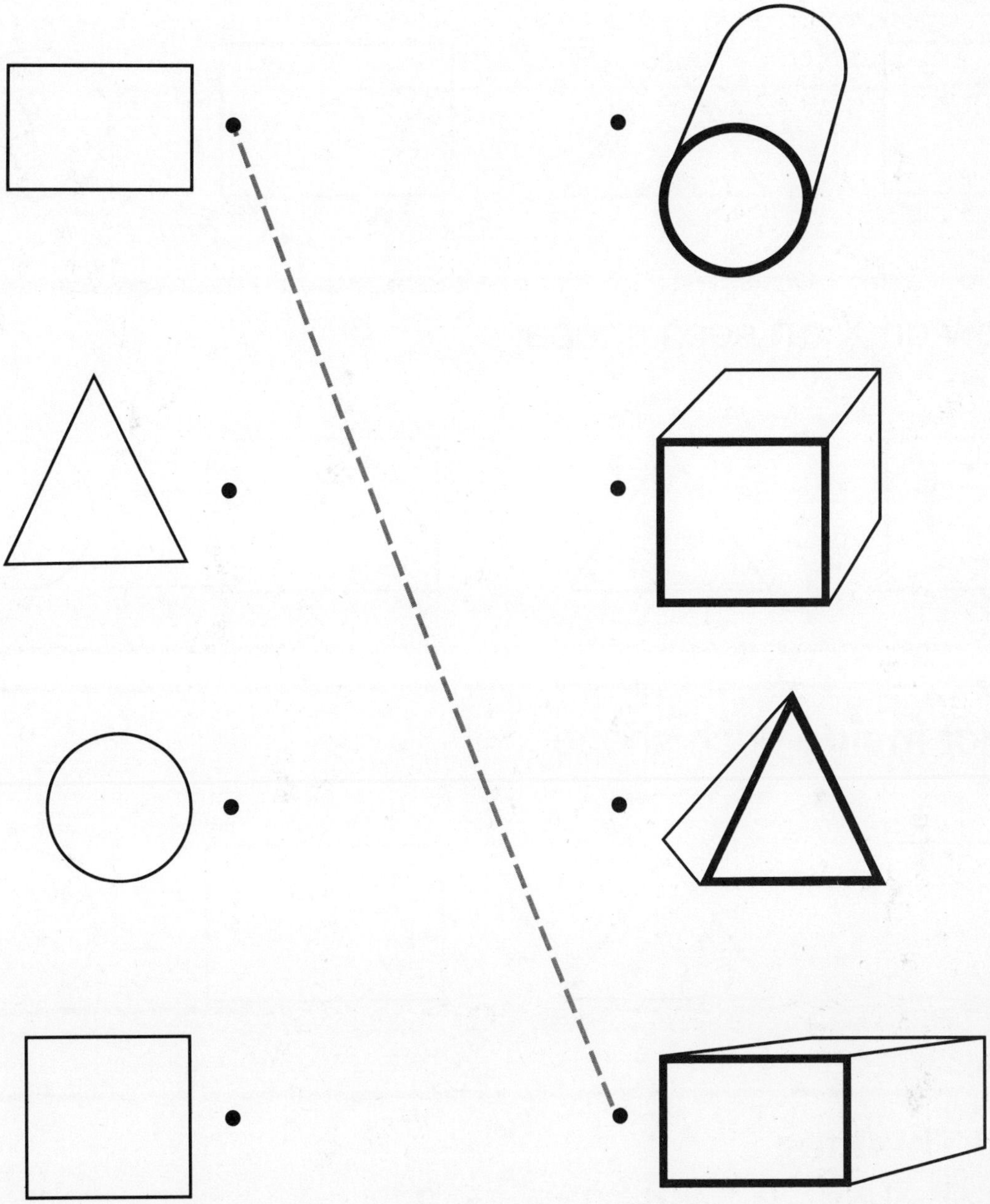

Visual Thinking

2. Count the △.
Write how many.

____

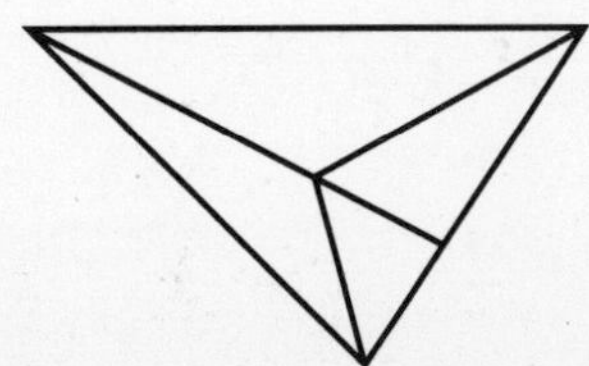

Name 

Inside, Outside, On

6.4
USE WHAT YOU KNOW

1. Draw an X **outside** each shape.

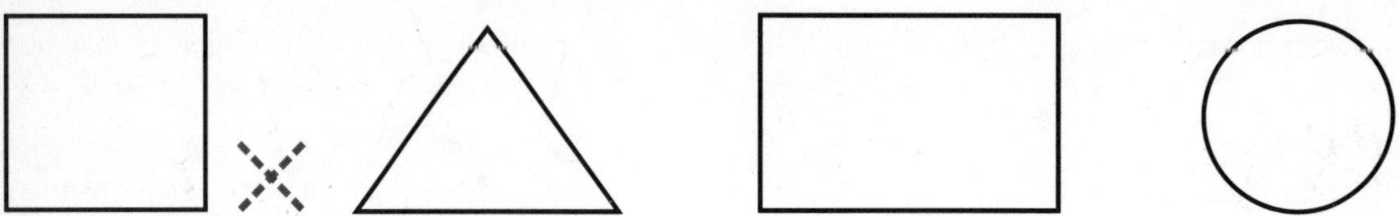

2. Draw an X **on** each shape.

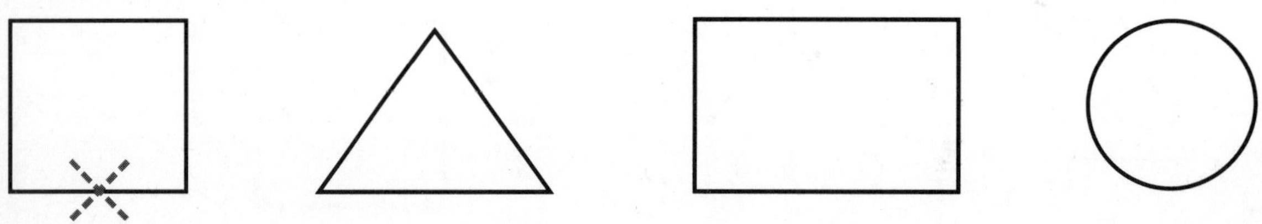

3. Color **inside** each shape.

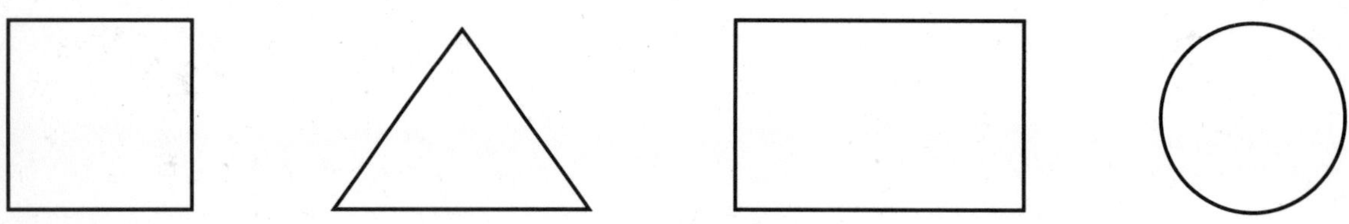

Visual Thinking

4. Which shape is inside 2 circles?
Ring the shape.

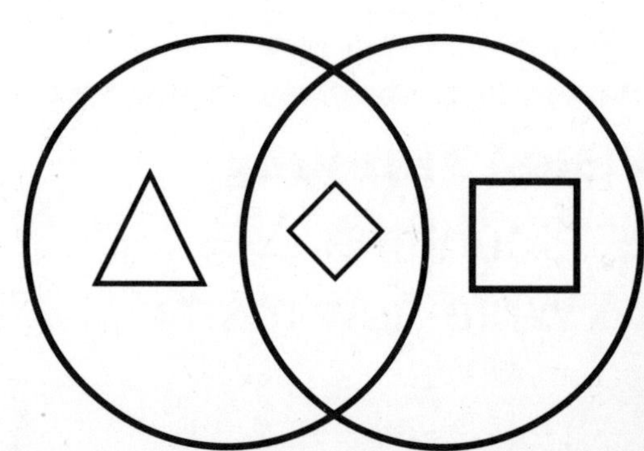

Use with text pages 165–166.

Name ______________________________________

6.5
USE WHAT YOU KNOW

Open and Closed Figures

Color inside each closed figure.
Ring the figures that are open.

open

closed

1.

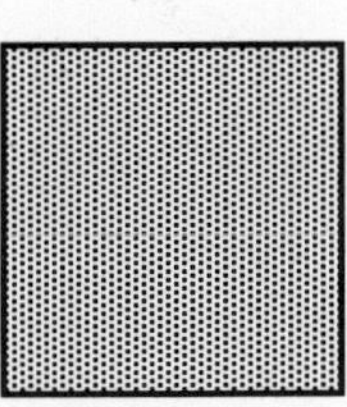

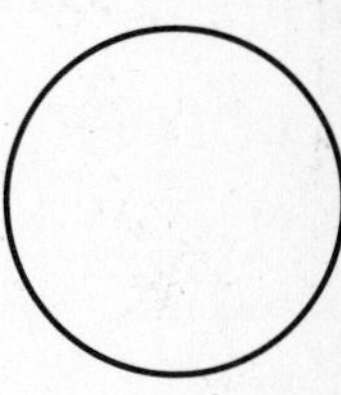

2.

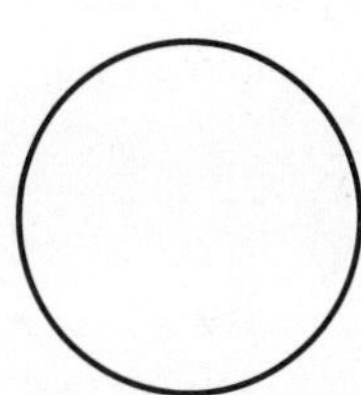
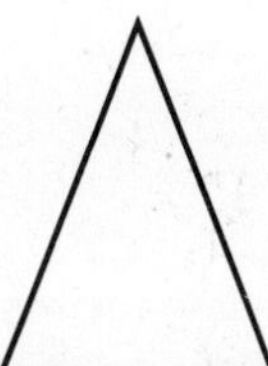

Color inside each rectangle.

3.

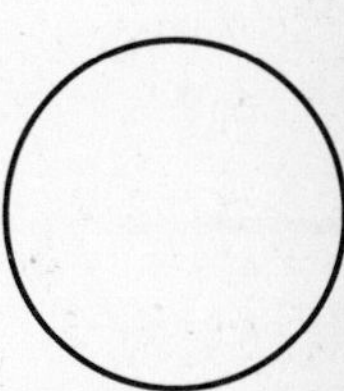

Visual Thinking

4. Ring the letters that are open figures.

C D G N O S

Name ____________________

6.6 USE WHAT YOU KNOW

Sides and Corners

Trace each side  .

Draw a 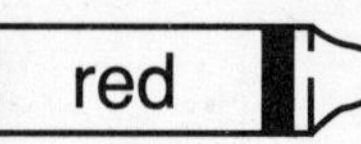 ◯ on each corner.

Write how many sides and corners.

1. 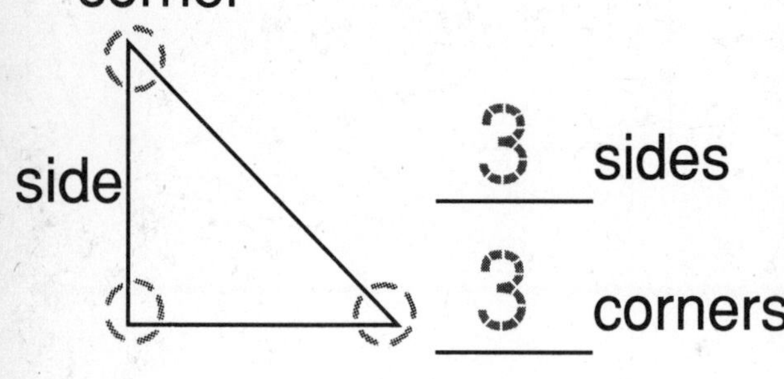

3 sides

3 corners

2. 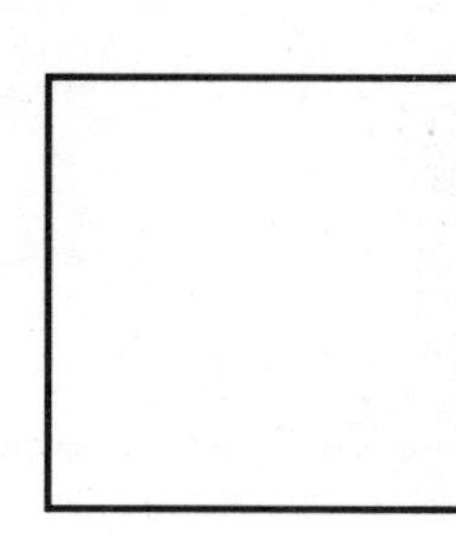

____ sides

____ corners

3. 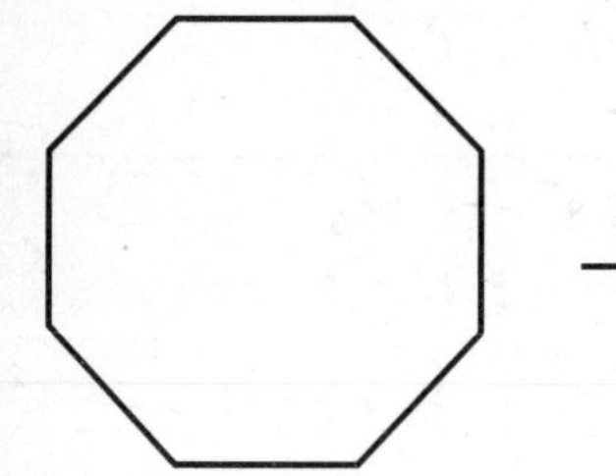

____ sides

____ corners

4. 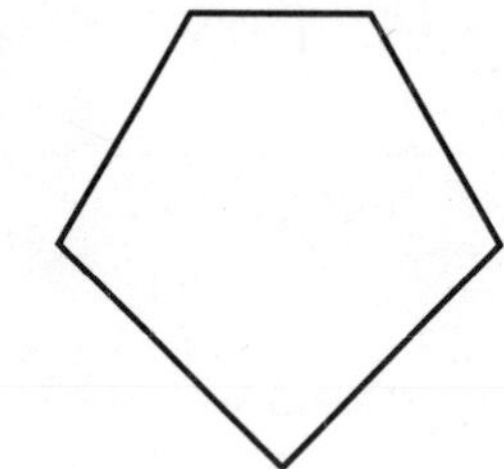

____ sides

____ corners

5. 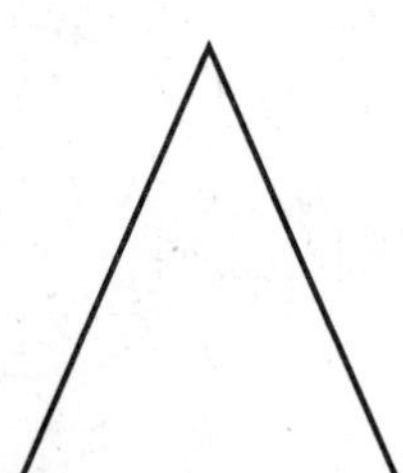

____ sides

____ corners

6. 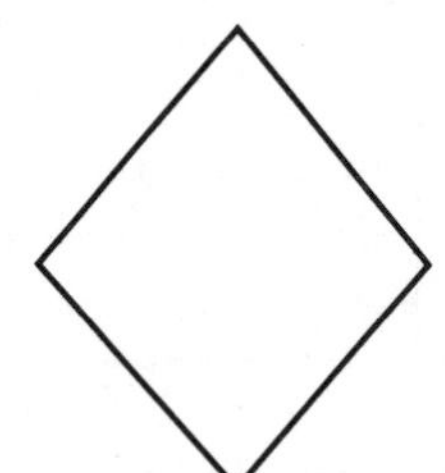

____ sides

____ corners

Reasoning

7. What kind of figure has 2 sides and 1 corner? Ring the answer.

open figure   closed figure

Use with text pages 169–170.

Name ______________________________

Problem-Solving Strategy

Make a Bar Graph

Count the shapes. Complete the graph.

1.

(cube)								
(cone)								
(cylinder)								
(rectangular prism)								
0	1	2	3	4	5	6	7	8

Story Corner

2. Read this riddle. Draw the shape.
   I am an open figure. I have 4 sides.
   I am a letter between T and X. ______

Use with text pages 171–172.

Name ____

6.8
USE WHAT YOU KNOW

Symmetry

Draw a line to make two parts that match.

1.
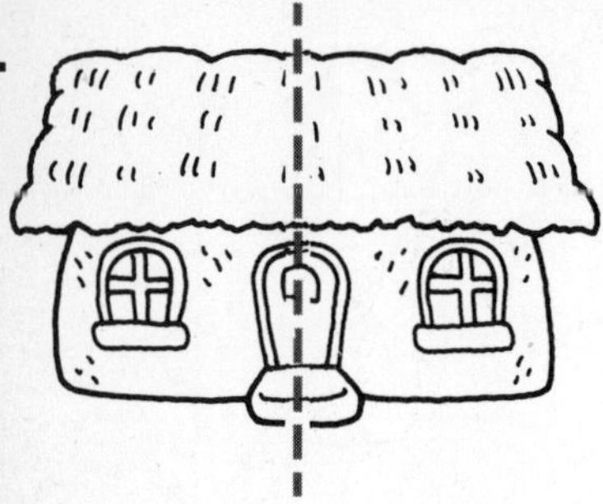

2.

3.
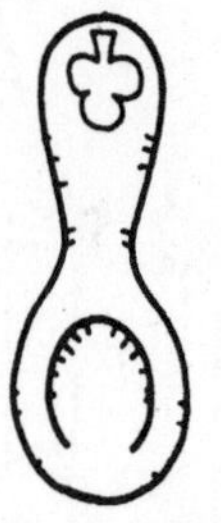

4.
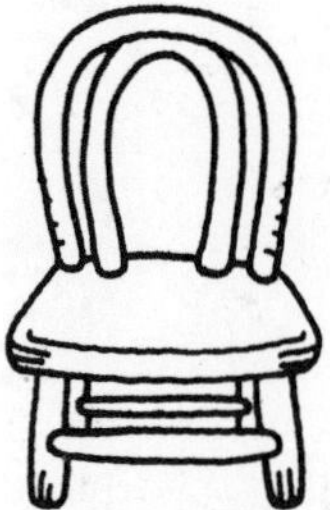

5.
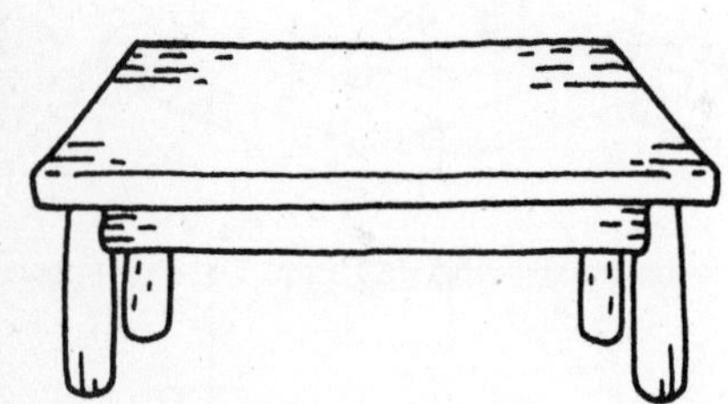

6.
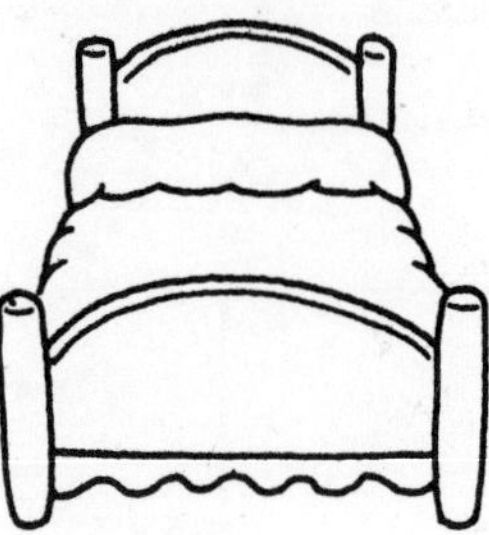

7.
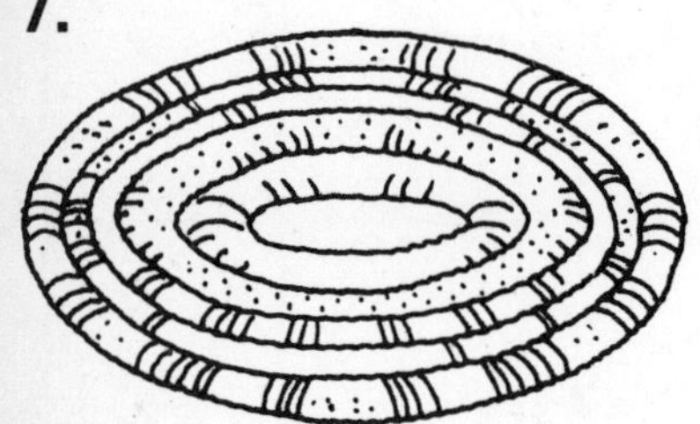

8.

Visual Thinking

9. Ring the two parts that do **not** match.

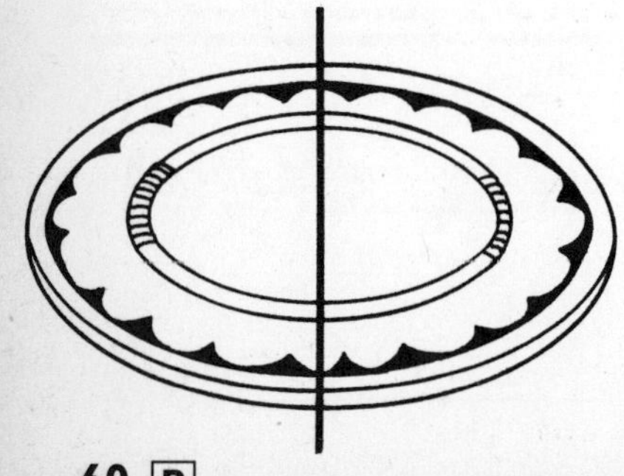

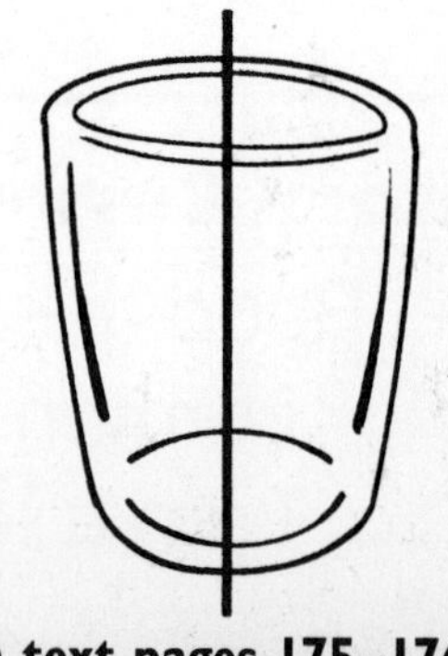

Use with text pages 175–176.

Name ______________________________

6.9 USE WHAT YOU KNOW

Congruent Figures

Ring the ones that are the same shape and size. Use punch-out shapes if you need to.

I.

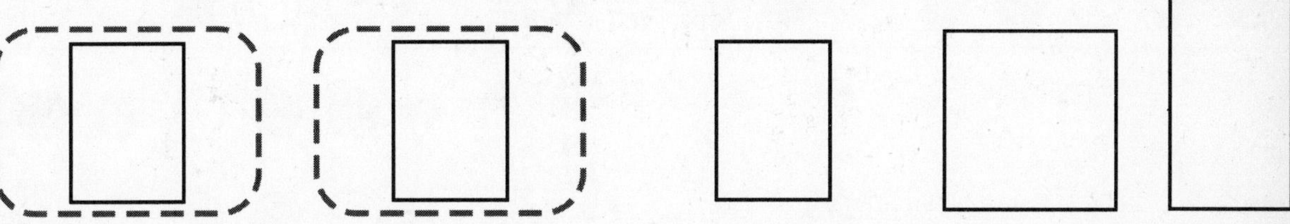

2.

3.

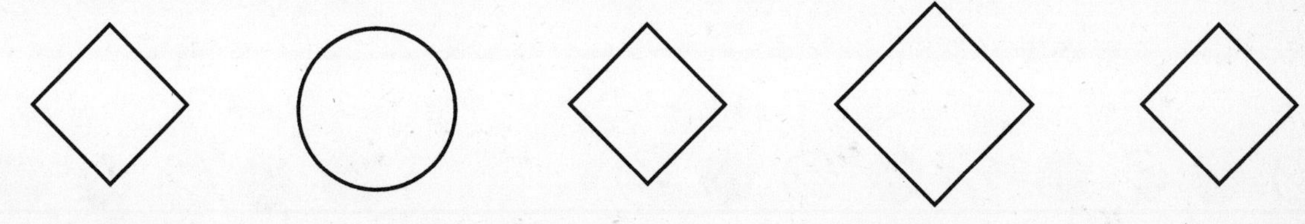

4.

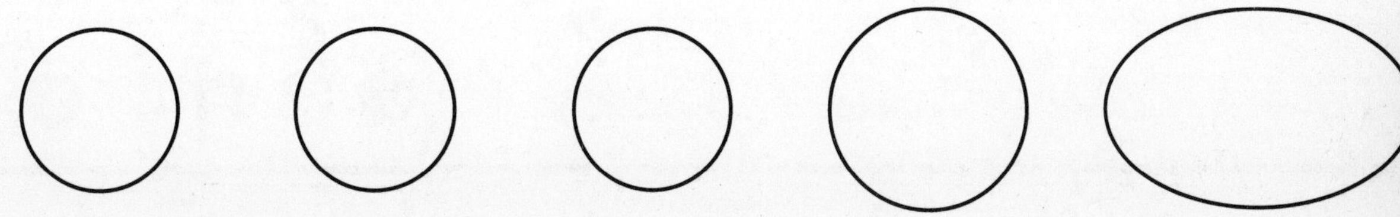

Story Corner

5. Compare the figures to the first one. Ring the correct word.

Same Smaller

Same Smaller

Same Bigger

Name ______________________________

6.10
USE WHAT YOU KNOW

Patterns

Match to continue each pattern.

1.

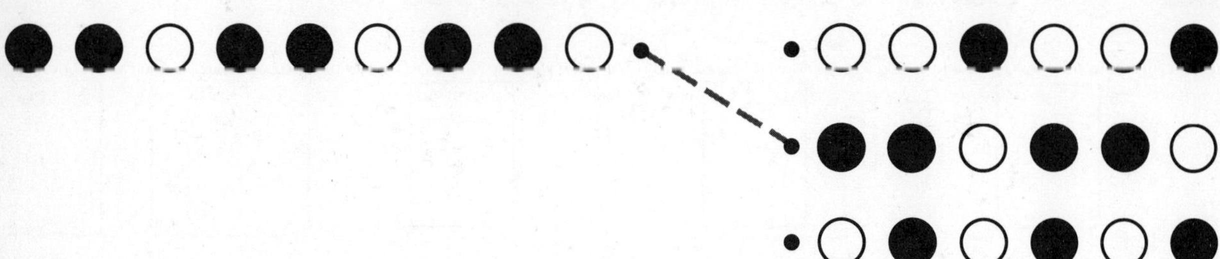

2.

3.

Number Sense

4. Draw a line under the row that shows a number pattern.

Use with text pages 179–180.

Name ________________________________

6.11
USE WHAT YOU KNOW

More Patterns

Color the stars to continue the pattern.

Color R stars red.

Color B stars blue.

1.

2.

3.

Number Sense

4. Write a number to continue the pattern.

4 1 2 4 1 2 4 1 2 4 ______

Name ____________________

6.12 USE WHAT YOU KNOW

Problem-Solving Strategy

Find a Pattern

Read each pattern. Color the pennant.

Color  .

Color  .

Color  .

1. 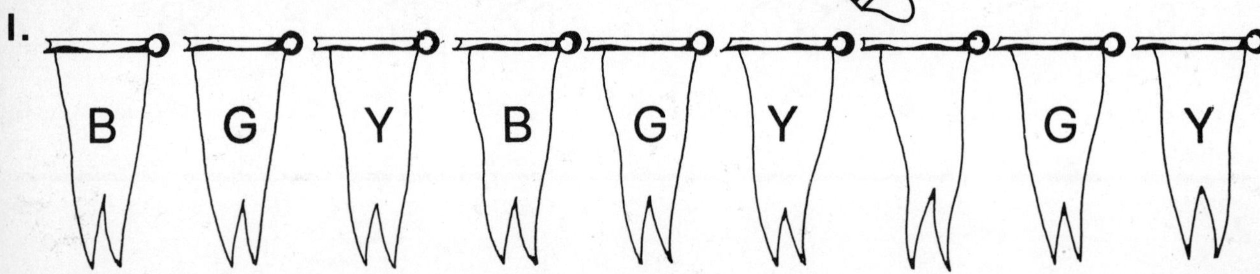

2. 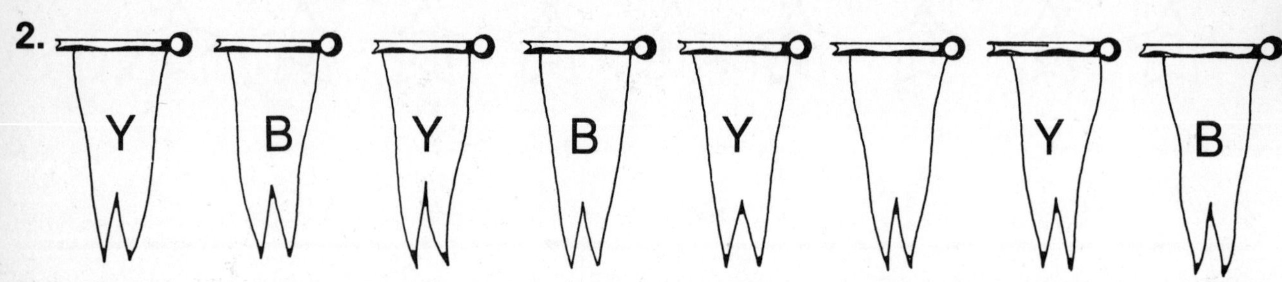

3. 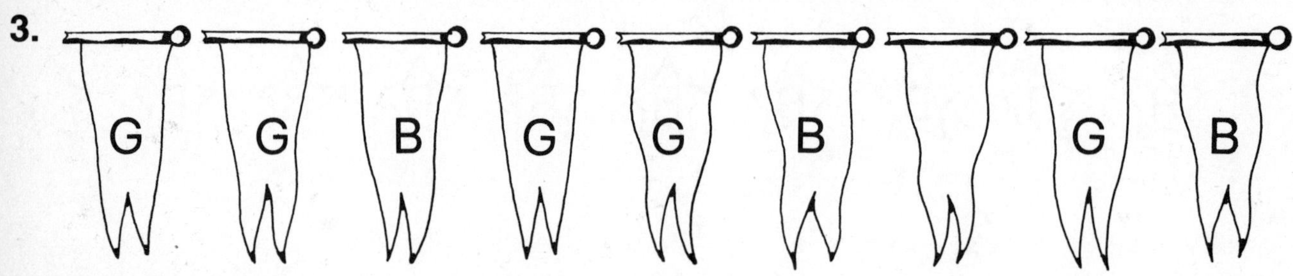

Number Sense

4. Ring the missing number.

9 2 9 2 9 ?

9 4 2

Use with text pages 183–184.

Name ______________________________

7.1 USE WHAT YOU KNOW

Groups of 10

Ring groups of 10.
Write how many groups you made.
Write how many in all.

1.

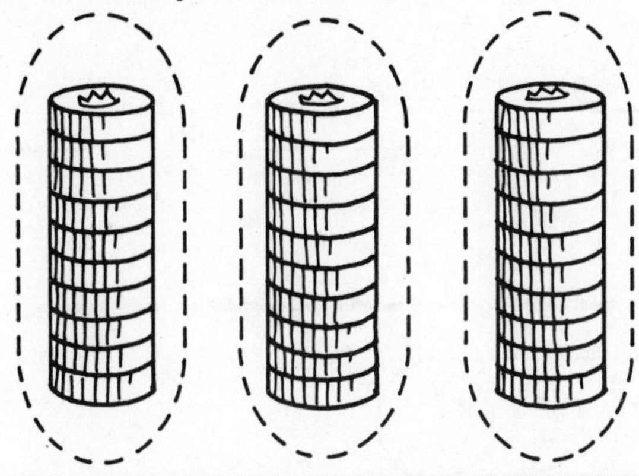

3 groups of 10

30

2.

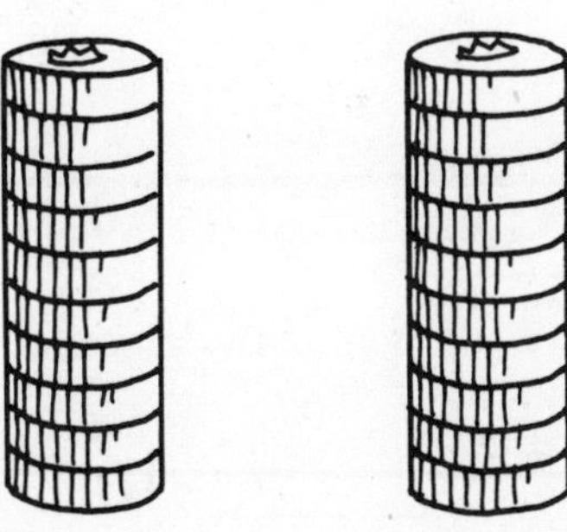

____ groups of 10

____

3.

____ groups of 10

____

Number Sense

4. Which group has the greater number? Ring it.

4 groups of 10

2 groups of 10

Name ___

Tens and Ones to 20

7.2
USE WHAT YOU KNOW

Use Workmat 3. Show each number.
Write how many.

1. 1 ten 1 one

11

2. ___ ten ___ ones

___

3. ___ ten ___ ones

___

4. ___ tens ___ ones

___

Number Sense

5. How many 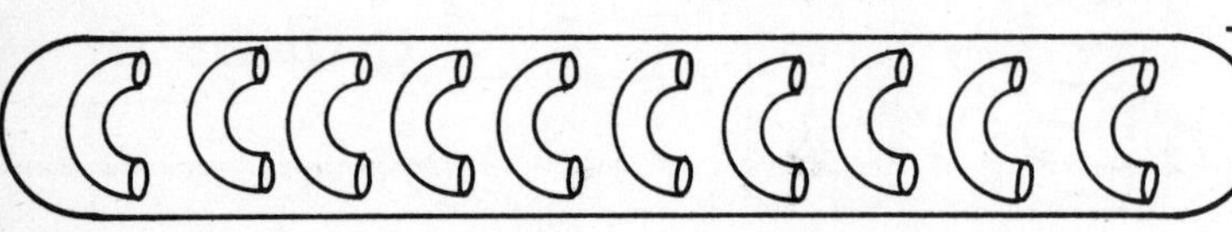 are there?
Ring the better estimate.

more than 10 fewer than 10

Use with text pages 197–198.

Name ______________________________

Tens and Ones to 50

Count. Write how many in all.

1.

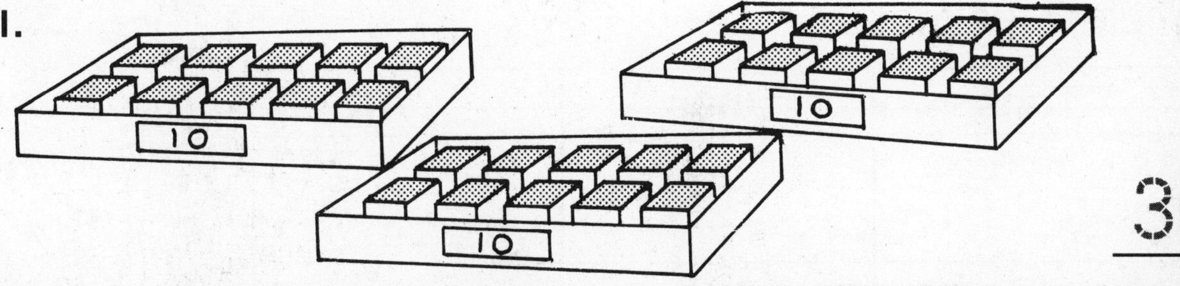

30

2.

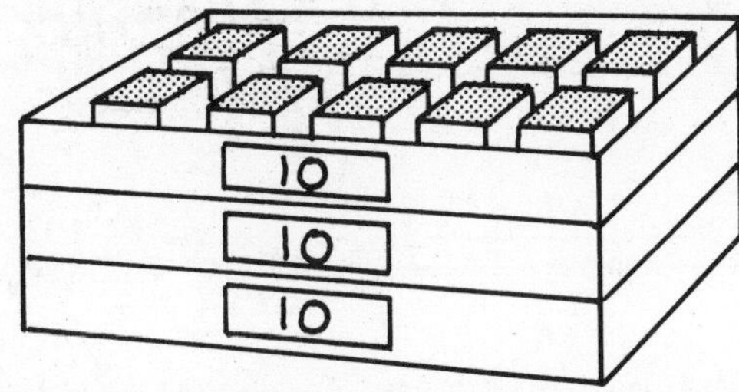

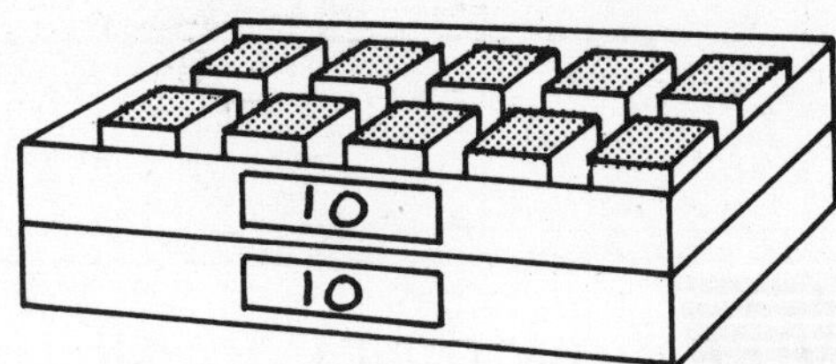

______

3.

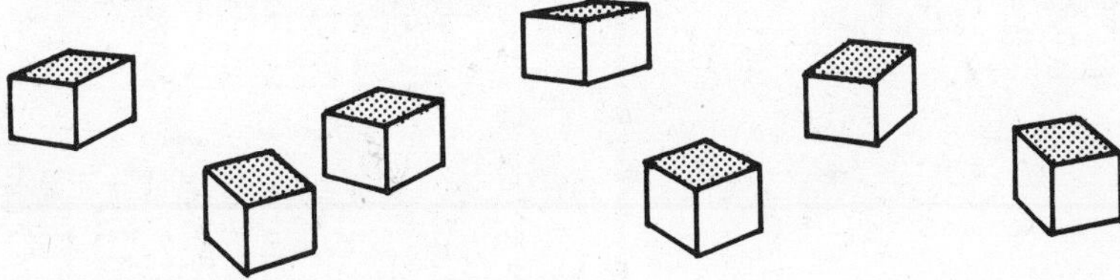

______

4.

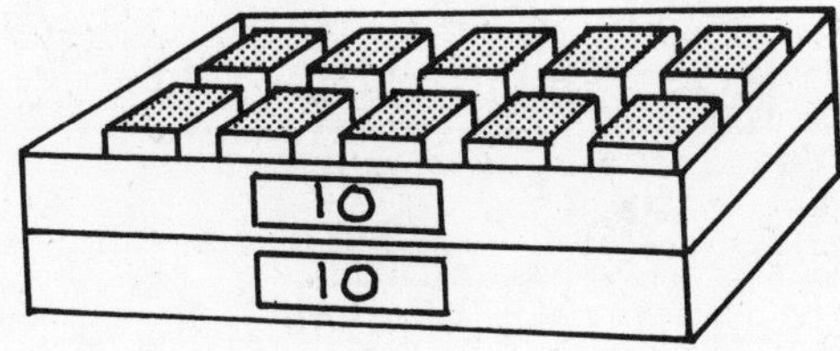

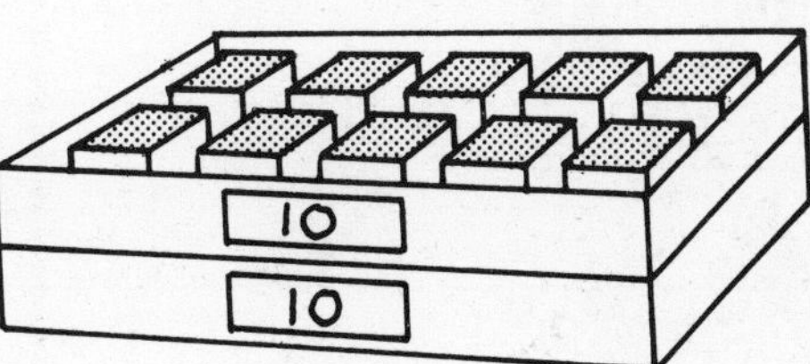

______

Problem Solving

5. The game has 20 white cubes.
It has 1 red cube.
How many cubes does the game have in all?

______ cubes

Name ____________________

Tens and Ones to 80

Use place-value models and Workmat 3.
Complete the table.

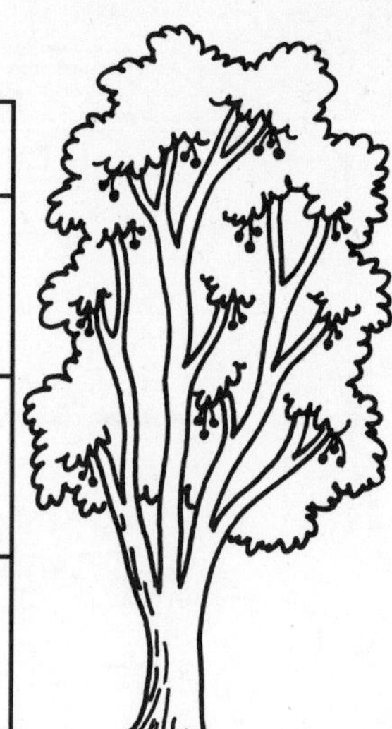

1.

Tens	Ones	In All
6	5	65
3	6	____
5	4	____

Count. Write how many in all.

2. 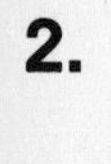   

36

3. 

____

4. 

____

5. 

____

Number Sense

6. Ring the group that has the greater number.

Use with text pages 201–202.

Name ____________________

Tens and Ones to 100

Use place-value models and Workmat 3.
Complete the table.

1.

Tens	Ones	In All
7	4	74
8	4	____
9	4	____

Count. Write how many in all.

2. 

65

3. 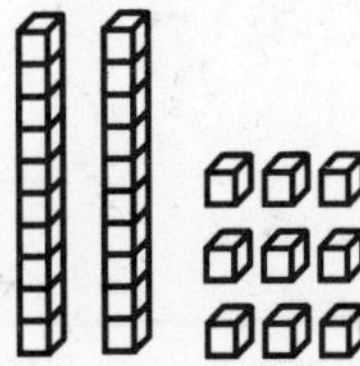

____

4. 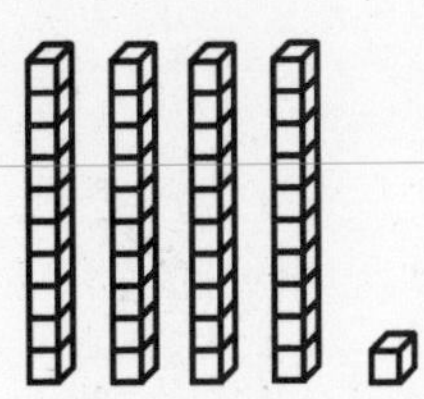

____

5. 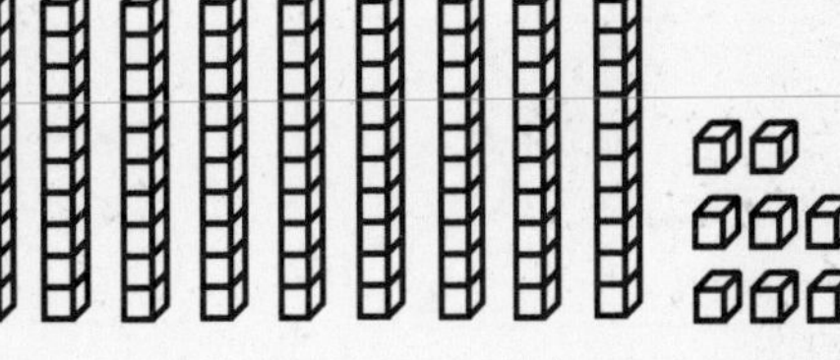

____

Number Sense

6. Ring the number that is less.

8 tens 6 ones   7 tens 6 ones

Name ______________________________

7.6
USE WHAT YOU KNOW

Problem-Solving Strategy

Use Estimation

Ring the best estimate.
Ring groups of 10 to check your estimate.

1.

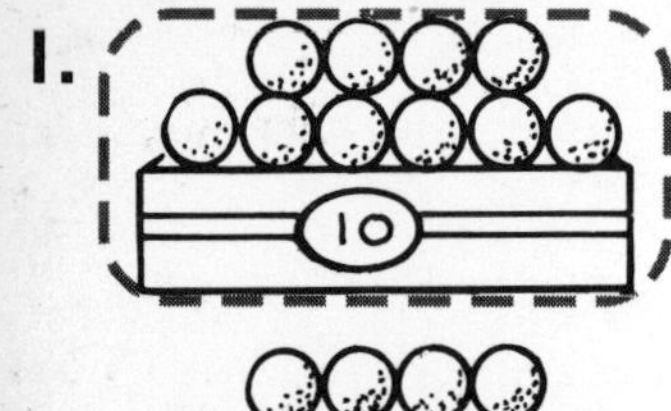
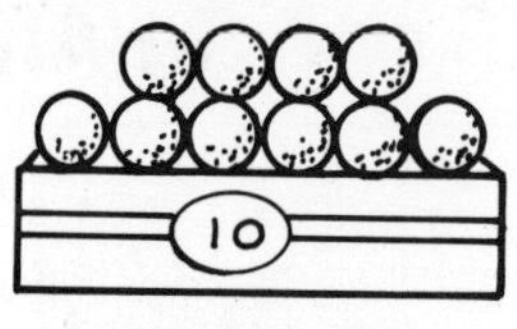
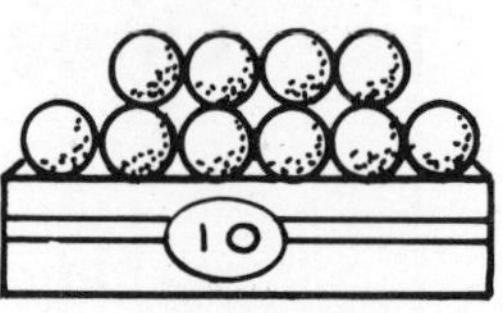
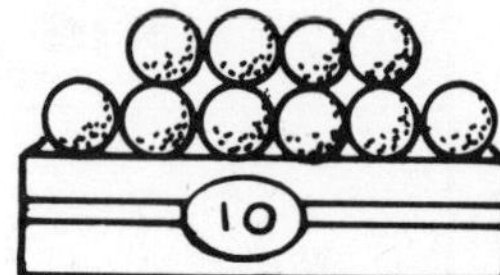
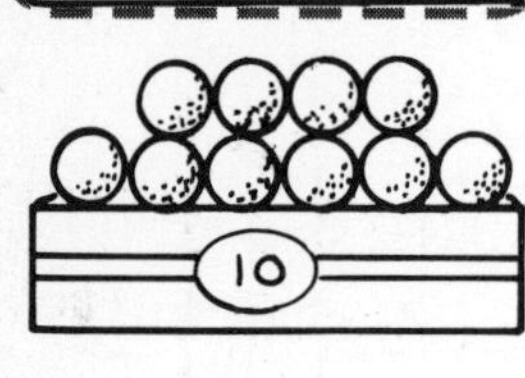
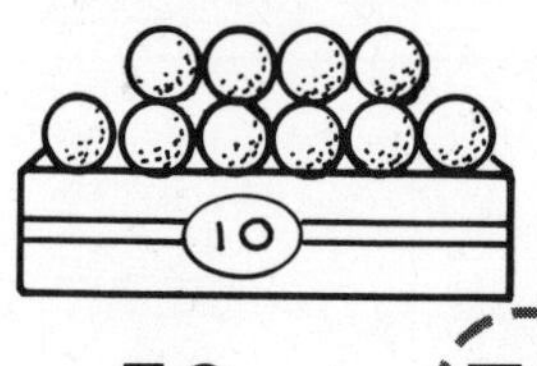
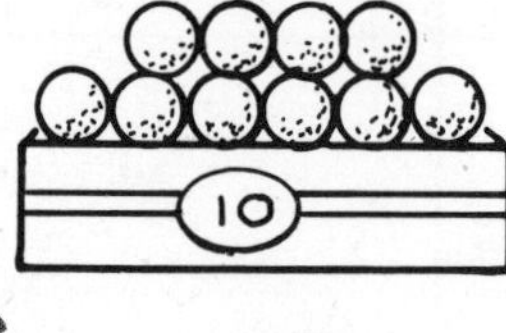
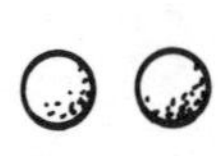

50 (70) 90

2.

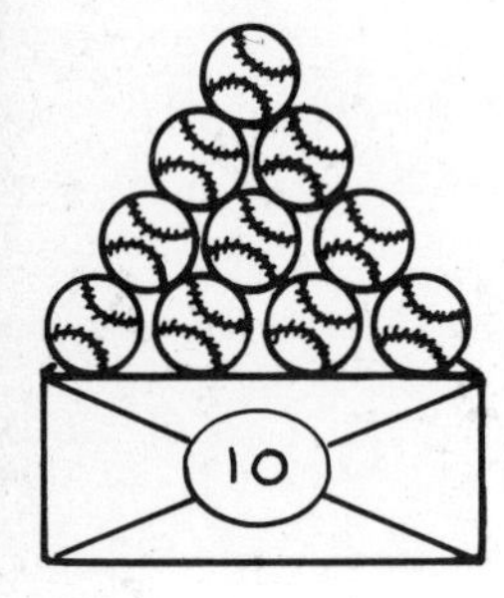
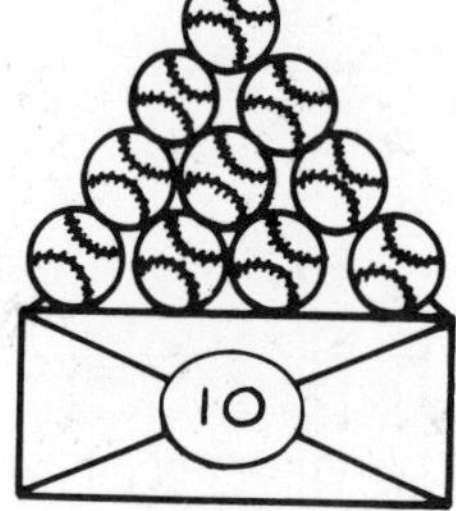

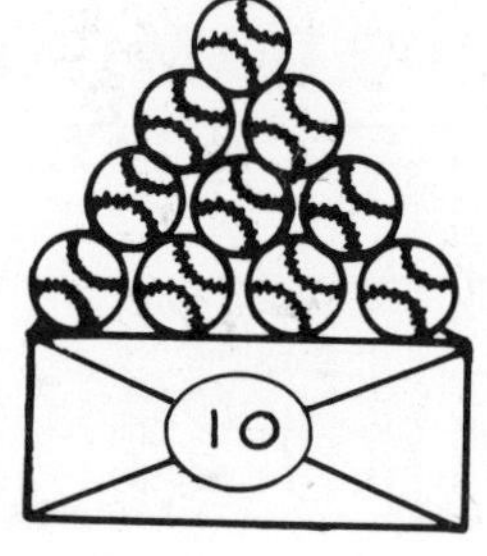

10 30 50

3.

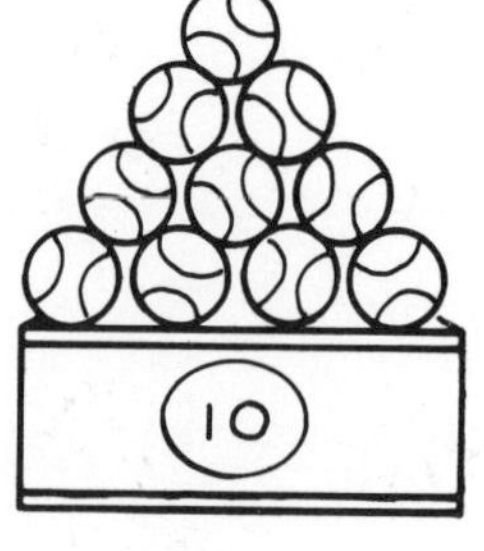
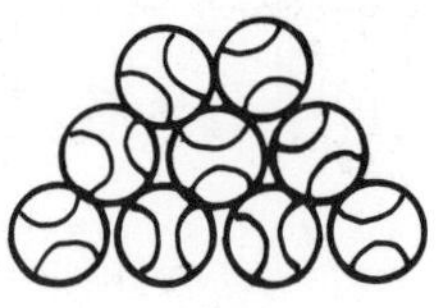

40 60 70

Reasoning

Write the answer.

4. Is 57 closer to 50 or to 60? ______

Use with text pages 205–206.

Name ______________________________

7.7
USE WHAT YOU KNOW

Counting Pennies

10 pennies

Count. Write how many pennies in all.

1.

12

2.

______

3.

______

4.

______

Number Sense

5. Ring the greater amount of money.

Use with text pages 209–210.

Name ____________________

7.8 USE WHAT YOU KNOW

Trading Groups

You will need 2 (dime).
Count the pennies. Ring groups of 10.
Put 1 dime on each group of 10.
Write how many dimes and pennies.

1.

__1__ dime __5__ pennies

2.

_____ dimes _____ pennies

Reasoning

3. Which money is easier to count?

Use with text pages 211–212.

Name ____

7.9 USE WHAT YOU KNOW

Comparing Numbers

Use place-value models and Workmat 3.
Ring the number that is greater. Use blue.

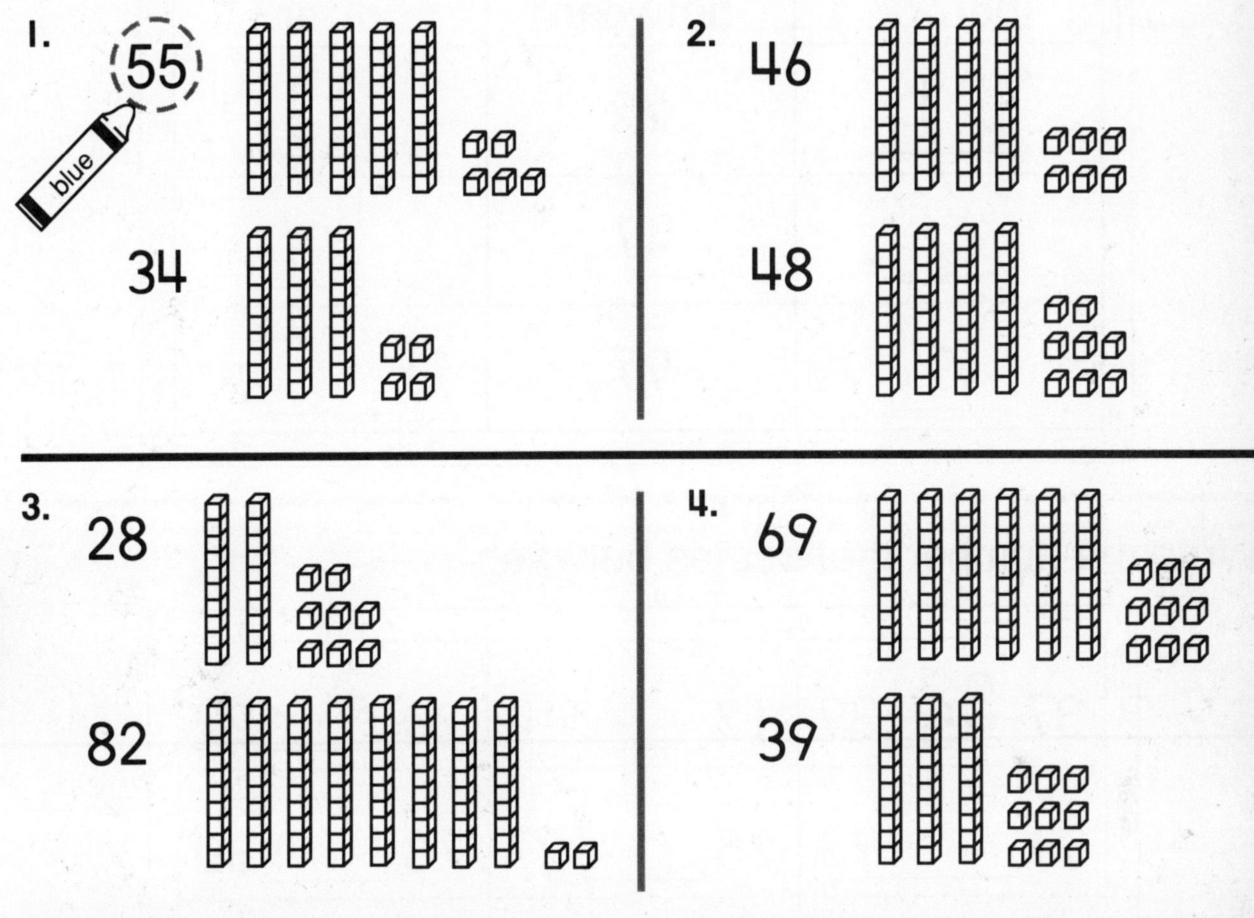

Number Sense

5. Which numbers are less than 50? Ring them in red.

34 78 12 99 41 56 29 21

50

73 22 44 20 38 63 92 85

Name ____________________

7.10 USE WHAT YOU KNOW

Before, After, Between

Use place-value models. Write the numbers.

1.

before	between	after
21	22	23
____	47	____
____	97	____

Write the number that comes between.

2.

37 38 39	12 ____ 14	20 ____ 22
91 ____ 93	25 ____ 27	78 ____ 80
22 ____ 24	86 ____ 88	32 ____ 34
61 ____ 63	44 ____ 46	80 ____ 82

Reasoning

Ring **Yes** or **No**.

3. Does 76 come before 77? Yes No

4. Is 76 less than 77? Yes No

Use with text pages 215–216.

Name ______________________________

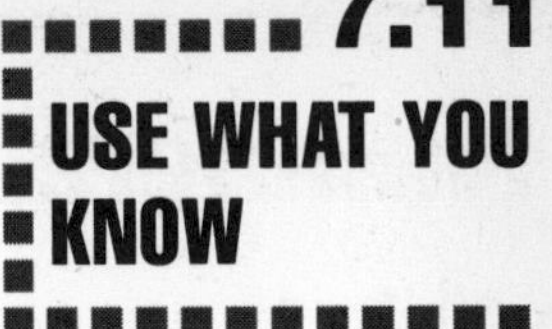

Order to 100

Write the missing numbers.

1. | 10 | 11 | 12 | 13 | | 15 | 16 | | 18 | |

2. | | 22 | 23 | | 25 | | | 28 | | 30 |

3. | 37 | | 39 | | | | 43 | | 45 | |

4. | 91 | | | 94 | 95 | 96 | | | | 100 |

5. | | 52 | | 54 | | | | 58 | 59 | |

Story Corner

Read this riddle. Write the numbers.

6. We are numbers between 81 and 86.
   We come after 83.

   ______ and ______

Name ______________________________

7.12
USE WHAT YOU KNOW

Numbers to 100

Write the missing numbers.

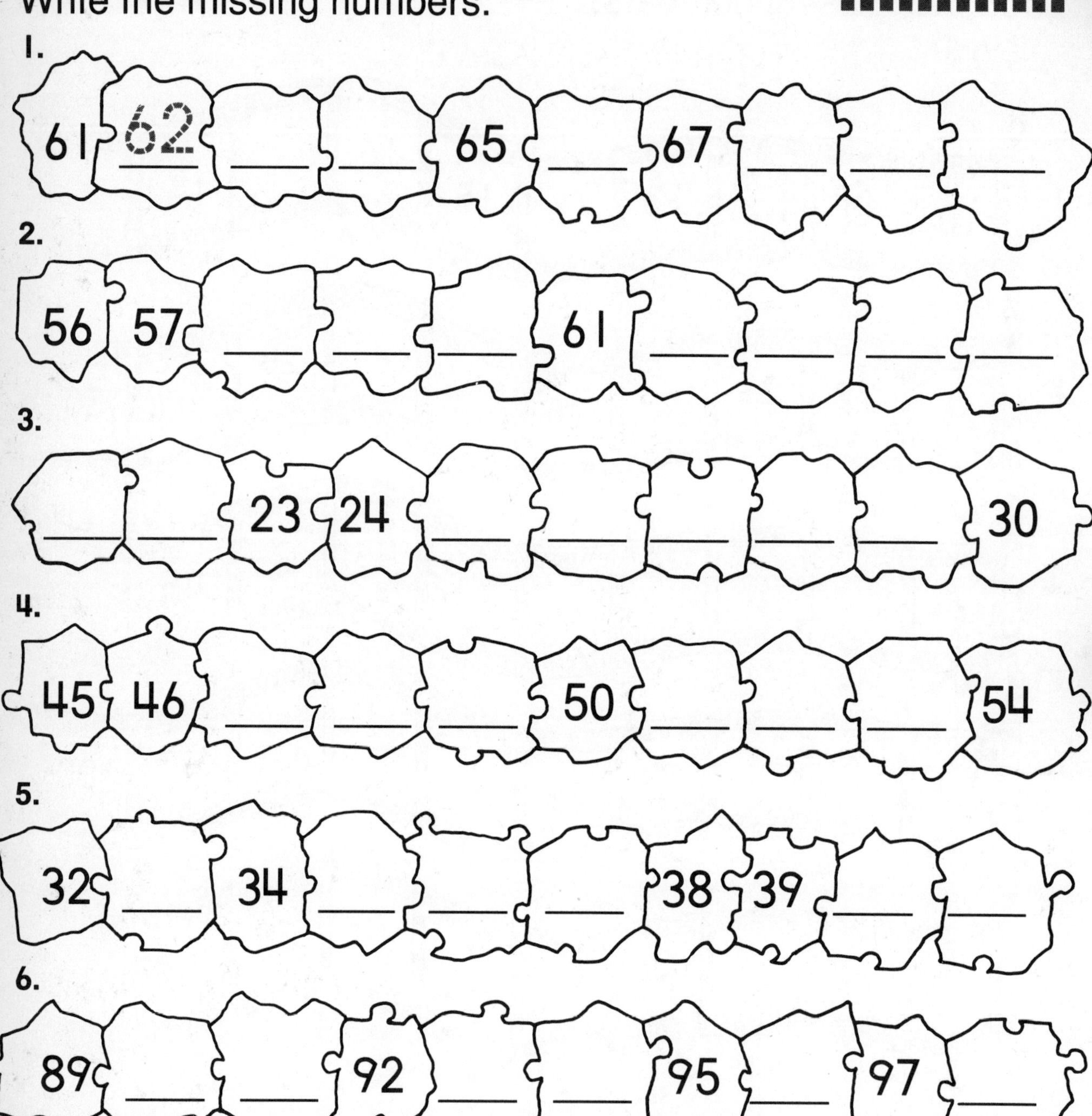

Number Sense

7. Ring the numbers that are less than 20.

15 16 17 18 19 20 21 22 23 24 25

Use with text pages 219–220.

Name ______________________________

Number Patterns

Use counters.

1. Stack 5 counters in each space.
   How many counters in all?

Count by fives.

5 ____ 10 ____ ____ ____ ____

2. Stack 10 counters in each space. How many counters in all?

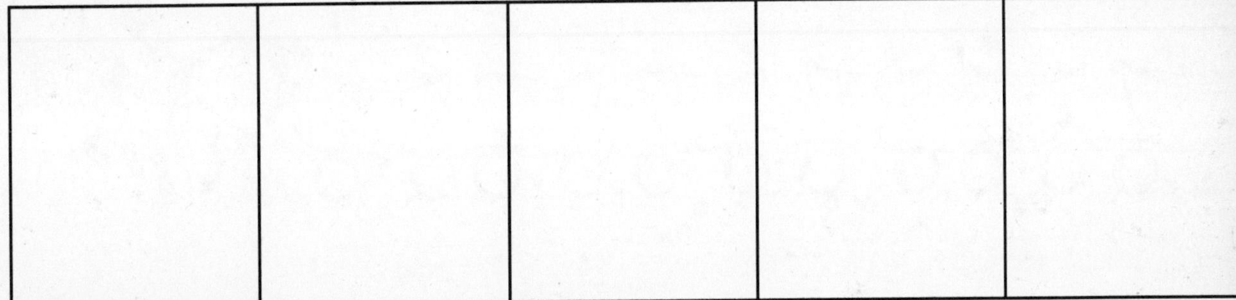

Count by tens.

10 ____ ____ ____ ____ ____

Number Sense

3. Write the missing number.

11	21	31	41	51	____

Name ______________________________

7.14
USE WHAT YOU KNOW

Ordinal Numbers

Match.

1.

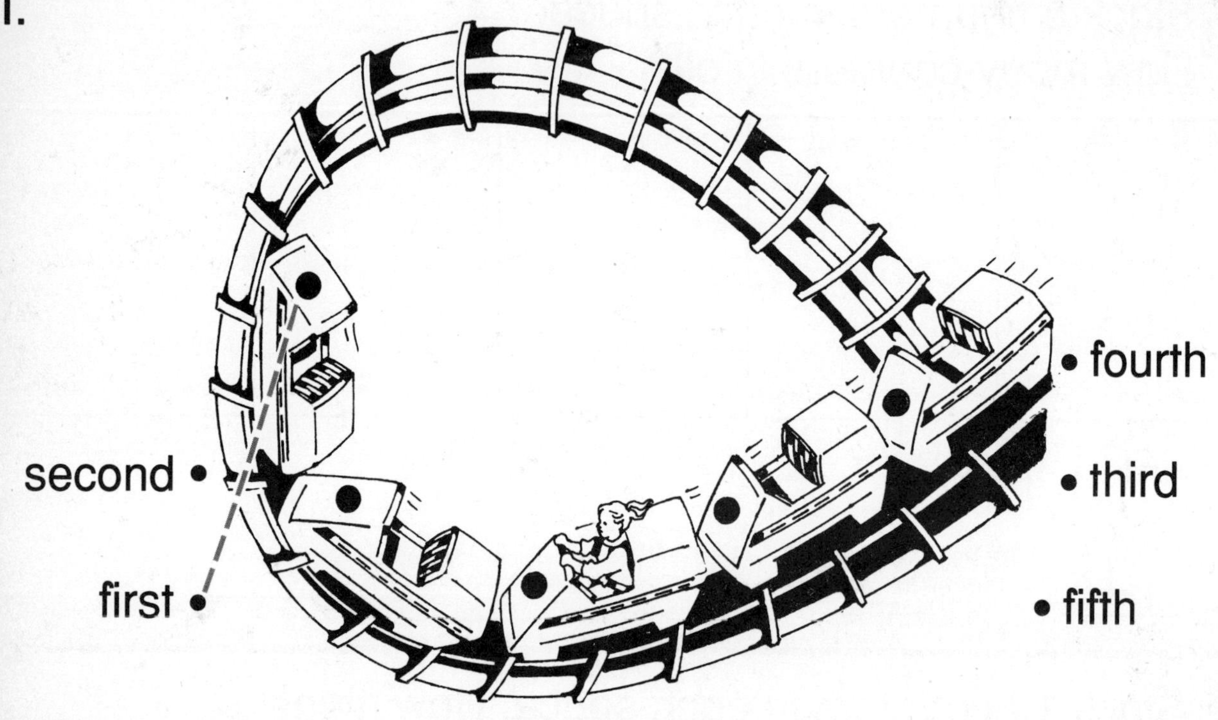

2.

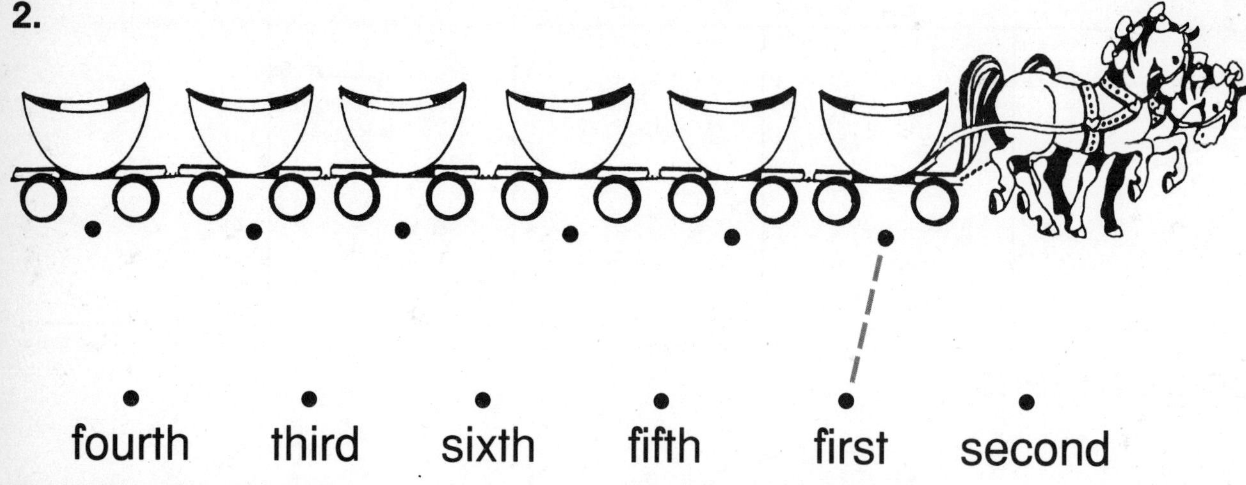

Reasoning

3. Which animal is first? Ring the answer.

rabbit duck can't tell

Use with text pages 223–224.

Name ______________________________________ **7.15**

USE WHAT YOU KNOW

Problem-Solving Strategy

Use a Pattern

Look for a pattern to answer each question.

1. How many marbles are in the fifth and sixth boxes?

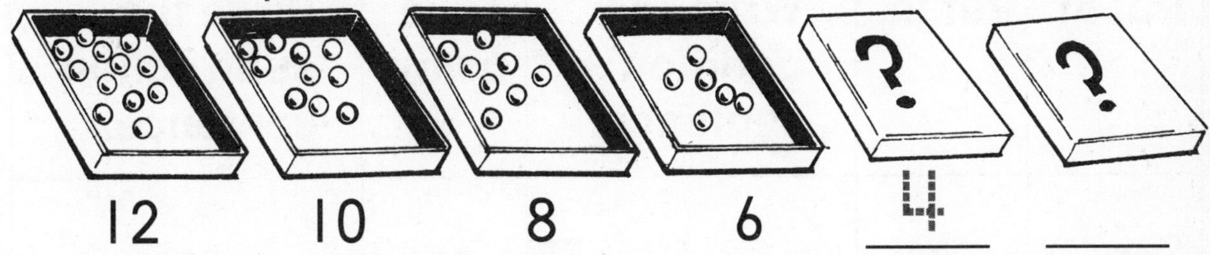

2. How many marbles are in the fifth, sixth and seventh boxes?

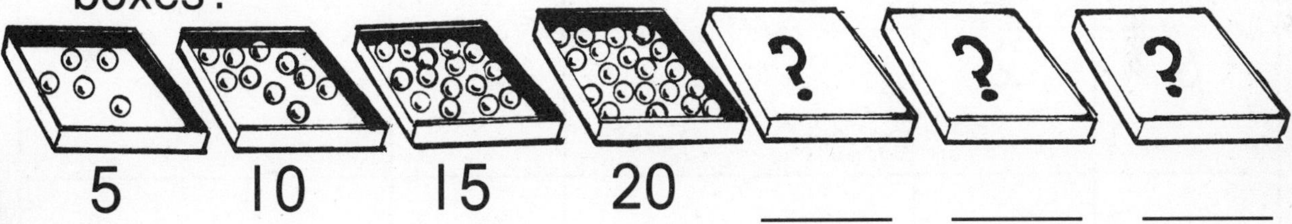

3. How many are in the last box?

______

Story Corner

4. Fran saves dimes every week.
   She uses the pattern below to save.
   How many dimes should she save in Week 4?

Week	1	2	3	4
Dimes	1	3	5	______

Name ______________________________

Adding and Subtracting

Work with a friend. You need connecting cubes and Workmat 1. Listen and do.

	Put in.	Put in.	Write the addition sentence.	Take away.	Write the subtraction sentence.
1.	3	4	3 + 4 = 7	4	7 − 4 = 3
2.	6	2		2	
3.	4	6		6	
4.	5	5		5	
5.	6	3		3	

Story Corner

6. Look at the picture.
Make up a story problem.
Tell it to a friend.
Write the number sentence. ____ ◯ ____ = ____

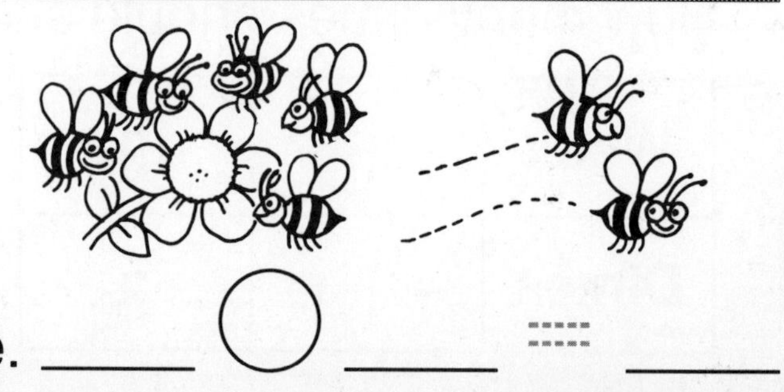

Use with text pages 235–236.

Name ________________________________

8.2 USE WHAT YOU KNOW

Counting On

Ring the greater number. Count on to add.

(7) + 1 = 8 (7, 8)	2 + (8) = 10 (8, 9, 10)	(8) + 3 = 11 (8, 9, 10, 11)

Ring the greater number. Write each sum.
Use counters to check.

1. (6) + 2 = 8   3 + 6   3 + 7   8 + 1   7 + 2   3 + 9

2. 1 + 9   9 + 2   2 + 8   3 + 5   8 + 3   5 + 2

3. 6 + 1   7 + 3   1 + 7   2 + 9   9 + 3   6 + 3

Reasoning

4. There are 10 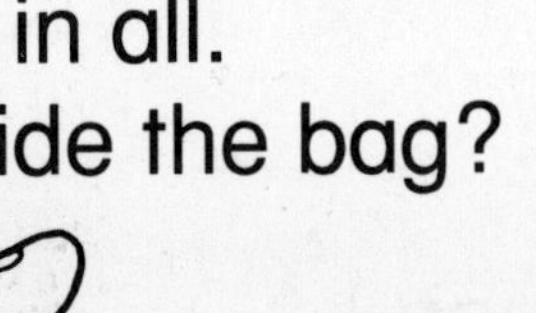 in all.
How many are inside the bag?

Name ____________________

8.3
USE WHAT YOU KNOW

Doubles

Ring each double. Write each sum.

1. (3 + 3) = 6 | 3 + 5 = ___ | 8 + 3 = ___

2. 4 + 2 = ___ | 6 + 6 = ___ | 4 + 4 = ___

3. 2 + 2 = ___ | 5 + 5 = ___ | 2 + 6 = ___

4. $\begin{array}{r} 1 \\ +1 \\ \hline \end{array}$ $\begin{array}{r} 1 \\ +7 \\ \hline \end{array}$ $\begin{array}{r} 3 \\ +7 \\ \hline \end{array}$ $\begin{array}{r} 2 \\ +8 \\ \hline \end{array}$ $\begin{array}{r} 3 \\ +3 \\ \hline \end{array}$ $\begin{array}{r} 6 \\ +3 \\ \hline \end{array}$

5. $\begin{array}{r} 5 \\ +3 \\ \hline \end{array}$ $\begin{array}{r} 5 \\ +5 \\ \hline \end{array}$ $\begin{array}{r} 4 \\ +4 \\ \hline \end{array}$ $\begin{array}{r} 2 \\ +7 \\ \hline \end{array}$ $\begin{array}{r} 8 \\ +3 \\ \hline \end{array}$ $\begin{array}{r} 6 \\ +6 \\ \hline \end{array}$

Problem Solving

Solve. Write the addition sentence.

6. The cow jumped over the moon 4 times.
Then it jumped 4 more times.
How many times did it jump in all?

___ + ___ = ___

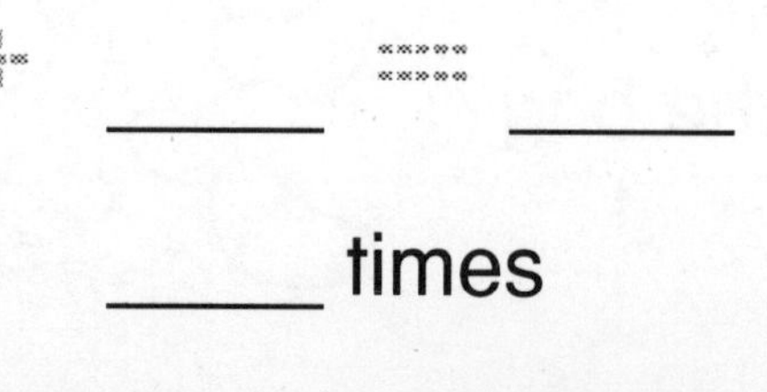

___ times

Use with text pages 239–240.

Name ______________________________

8.4
USE WHAT YOU KNOW

Doubles Plus One

Add.
Use counters if you need to.

1.	5	5	2	1	4	1
	+5	+6	+3	+1	+4	+2
	10					
2.	4	3	0	3	2	0
	+5	+3	+0	+4	+2	+1

Number Sense

Do each one in your head.
Then write the sum.

3. 4 + 4 = 8,
so 4 + 5 = 9

4. 0 + 0 = 0,
so 0 + 1 = ____

5. 2 + 2 = 4,
so 2 + 3 = ____

6. 1 + 1 = 2,
so 1 + 2 = ____

7. 5 + 5 = 10,
so 5 + 6 = ____

8. 3 + 3 = 6,
so 3 + 4 = ____

Name ____________________

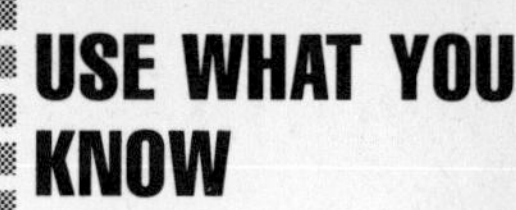

Order of Addends

$$\begin{array}{r} 7 \\ +3 \\ \hline 10 \end{array} \qquad \begin{array}{r} 3 \\ +7 \\ \hline 10 \end{array}$$

I see 4 and 4. That makes 8, and 1 more makes 9.

$$\begin{array}{r} 5 \\ +4 \\ \hline 9 \end{array} \qquad \begin{array}{r} 4 \\ +5 \\ \hline 9 \end{array}$$

Add.

1. $\begin{array}{r} 8 \\ +2 \\ \hline \end{array}$ $\begin{array}{r} 2 \\ +8 \\ \hline \end{array}$ $\begin{array}{r} 5 \\ +5 \\ \hline \end{array}$ $\begin{array}{r} 5 \\ +6 \\ \hline \end{array}$ $\begin{array}{r} 8 \\ +1 \\ \hline \end{array}$ $\begin{array}{r} 1 \\ +8 \\ \hline \end{array}$

2. $\begin{array}{r} 3 \\ +3 \\ \hline \end{array}$ $\begin{array}{r} 9 \\ +3 \\ \hline \end{array}$ $\begin{array}{r} 4 \\ +4 \\ \hline \end{array}$ $\begin{array}{r} 3 \\ +9 \\ \hline \end{array}$ $\begin{array}{r} 9 \\ +2 \\ \hline \end{array}$ $\begin{array}{r} 2 \\ +9 \\ \hline \end{array}$

Visual Thinking

3. Ring the correct answer.

10

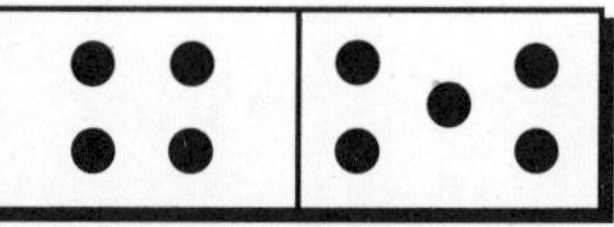

more than 10

less than 10

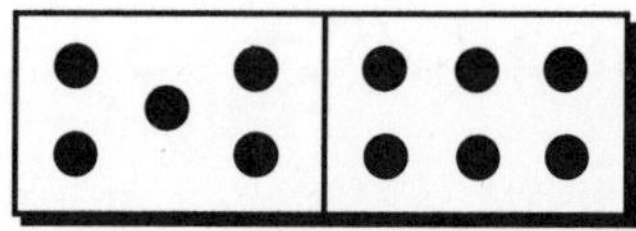

more than 10

less than 10

Use with text pages 243–244.

Name ______________________________

8.6
USE WHAT YOU KNOW

Problem-Solving Strategy

Make and Use a Bar Graph

Work with a group of ten classmates. Ask which animal each classmate in the group likes best. Use tally marks 𝍸 to count.

Color a ☐ for each tally mark.

1.

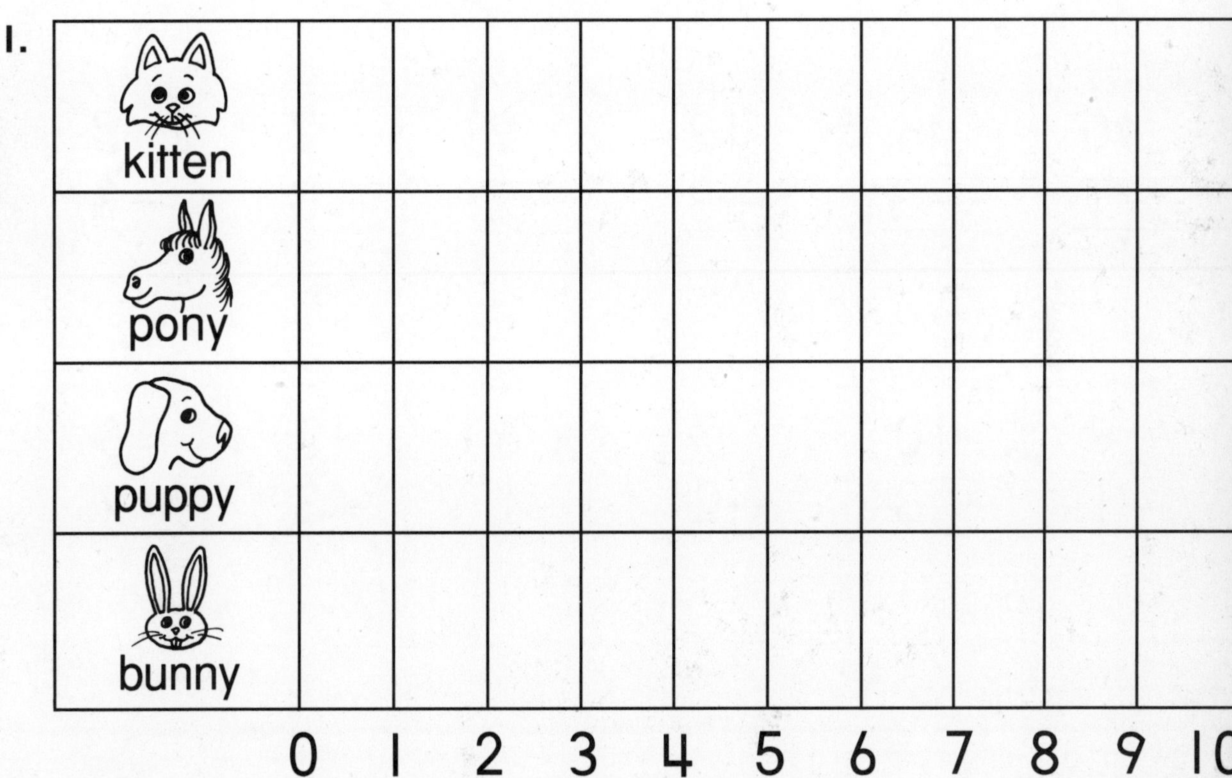

2. Which animal did your group like best? ______________
3. How many in your group chose this animal? ______________
4. Which animal did your group like the least? ______________

Name ______________________________

8.7

USE WHAT YOU KNOW

Counting Back

$$\begin{array}{r} 10 \\ -1 \\ \hline 9 \end{array}$$ (10, 9)

$$\begin{array}{r} 11 \\ -3 \\ \hline 8 \end{array}$$ (11, 10, 9, 8)

$$\begin{array}{r} 10 \\ -2 \\ \hline 8 \end{array}$$ (10, 9, 8)

Count back to subtract.

1. $\begin{array}{r} 11 \\ -2 \\ \hline \end{array}$ $\begin{array}{r} 8 \\ -1 \\ \hline \end{array}$ $\begin{array}{r} 9 \\ -3 \\ \hline \end{array}$ $\begin{array}{r} 7 \\ -1 \\ \hline \end{array}$ $\begin{array}{r} 8 \\ -3 \\ \hline \end{array}$ $\begin{array}{r} 10 \\ -2 \\ \hline \end{array}$

2. $\begin{array}{r} 10 \\ -1 \\ \hline \end{array}$ $\begin{array}{r} 11 \\ -3 \\ \hline \end{array}$ $\begin{array}{r} 12 \\ -3 \\ \hline \end{array}$ $\begin{array}{r} 9 \\ -2 \\ \hline \end{array}$ $\begin{array}{r} 7 \\ -3 \\ \hline \end{array}$ $\begin{array}{r} 8 \\ -2 \\ \hline \end{array}$

3. $\begin{array}{r} 9 \\ -1 \\ \hline \end{array}$ $\begin{array}{r} 10 \\ -3 \\ \hline \end{array}$ $\begin{array}{r} 7 \\ -2 \\ \hline \end{array}$ $\begin{array}{r} 6 \\ -1 \\ \hline \end{array}$ $\begin{array}{r} 12 \\ -3 \\ \hline \end{array}$ $\begin{array}{r} 6 \\ -2 \\ \hline \end{array}$

Reasoning

4. Which has the greatest difference? Ring it.

$\begin{array}{r} 50 \\ -3 \\ \hline \end{array}$ $\begin{array}{r} 50 \\ -2 \\ \hline \end{array}$ $\begin{array}{r} 50 \\ -1 \\ \hline \end{array}$

Use with text pages 249–250.

Name ______________________

8.8 USE WHAT YOU KNOW

Counting Up

Count up to subtract.

1. $8 - 7$ 7,8 (1 more) | $11 - 8$ 8,9,10,11 (3 more) | $7 - 5$ 6,7,8 (2 more) | $10 - 7$ 7,8,9,10 (3 more)

2. $11 - 9$ (9,10,11) | $10 - 8$ (8,9,10) | $9 - 8$ (8,9) | $12 - 9$ (9,10,11,12)

3. $10 - 9$ | $8 - 6$ | $6 - 5$ | $7 - 4$ | $9 - 7$ | $5 - 3$

4. $12 - 8$ | $5 - 2$ | $7 - 6$ | $10 - 8$ | $8 - 5$ | $6 - 4$

Reasoning

Use counting back or counting up to subtract.

5. $11 - 8$ | $12 - 3$ | $9 - 6$ | $10 - 2$ | $8 - 1$ | $8 - 6$

Ring in red the counting up facts.
Ring in blue the counting back facts.

Name ____________________

Addition and Subtraction

Add. Then subtract.
Use counters to show.

1. 6 + 5 = 11
   11 − 5 = 6

2. 7 + 4 = ____
   11 − 4 = ____

3. 5 + 5 = ____
   10 − 5 = ____

4. 8 + 4 = ____
   12 − 4 = ____

5. 9 + 2 = ____
   11 − 2 = ____

6. 6 + 6 = ____
   12 − 6 = ____

7. 7 + 3 = ____
   10 − 3 = ____

8. 7 + 5 = ____
   12 − 5 = ____

Problem Solving

Ring **Add** or **Subtract**.

9. A pieman made 8 pies. Then he made 4 more. How many did he make in all?

   Add   Subtract

Name ______________________________

8.10
USE WHAT YOU KNOW

Fact Families

Add or subtract. Ring the sentence that does not belong.

1.

3 + 7 = 10

7 + 3 = 10

6 + 3 = 9

10 − 7 = 3

10 − 3 = 7

2.

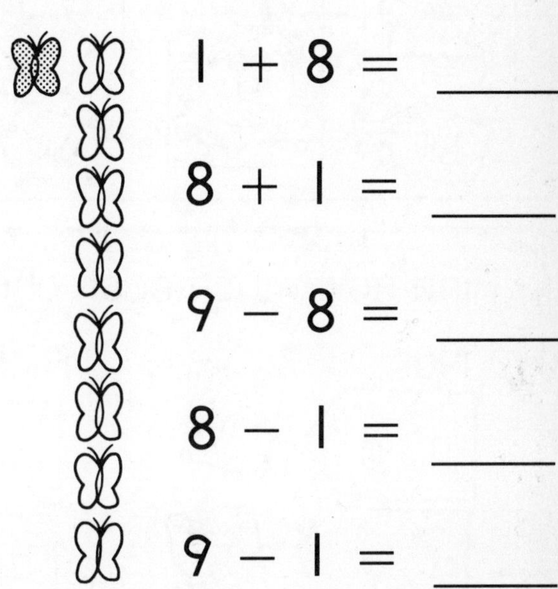

1 + 8 = ____

8 + 1 = ____

9 − 8 = ____

8 − 1 = ____

9 − 1 = ____

3.

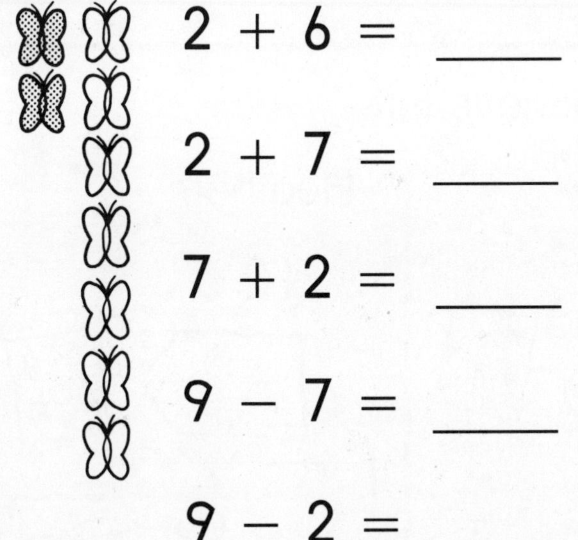

2 + 6 = ____

2 + 7 = ____

7 + 2 = ____

9 − 7 = ____

9 − 2 = ____

4.

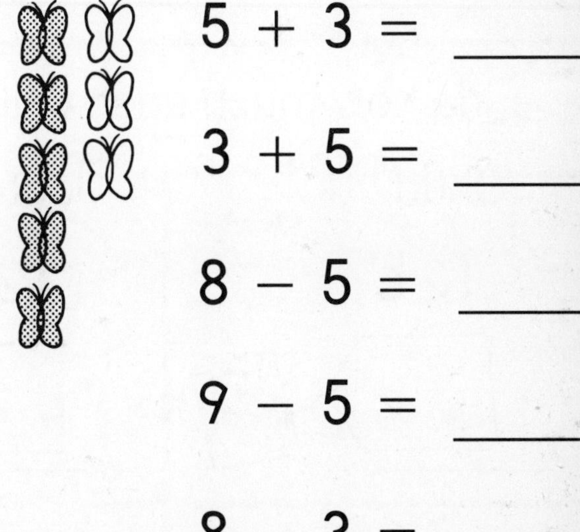

5 + 3 = ____

3 + 5 = ____

8 − 5 = ____

9 − 5 = ____

8 − 3 = ____

Reasoning

5. Write the difference.

13 − 5 = 8, so 13 − 8 = ____

Name ______________________________

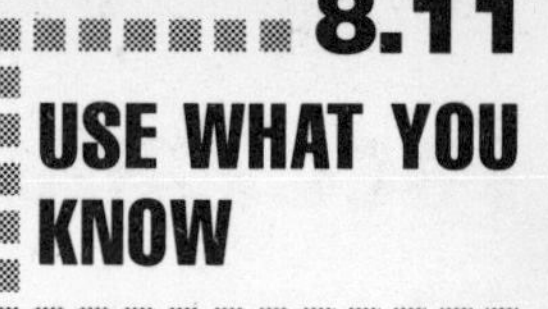

Using Pennies

1. Find how much each child spent.

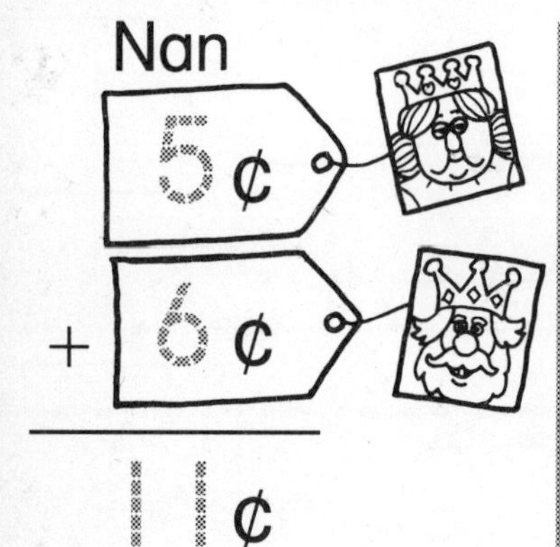

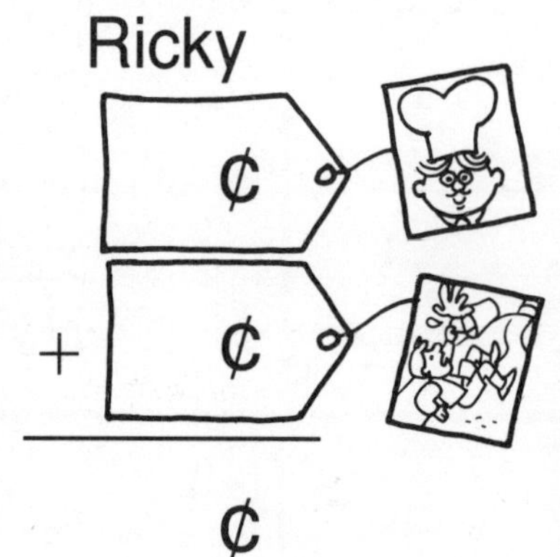

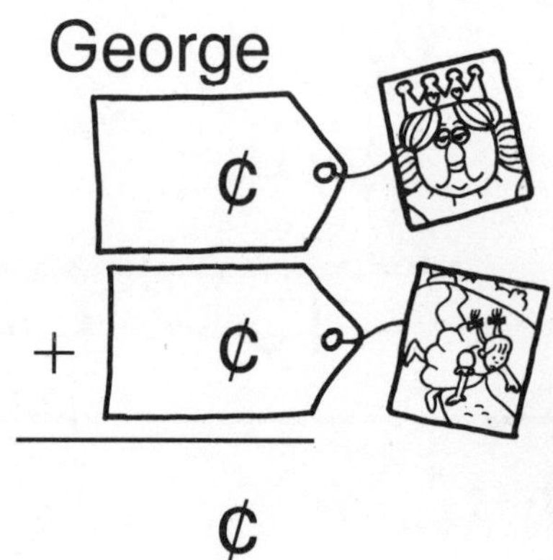

2. Find how much each child will have left.

Chad

12 ¢
− 7 ¢
5 ¢

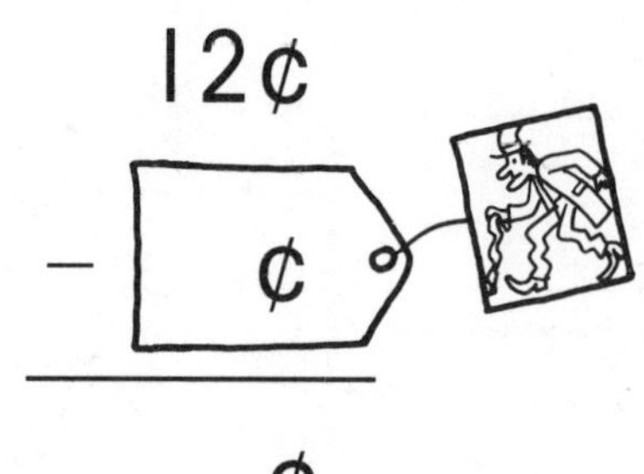

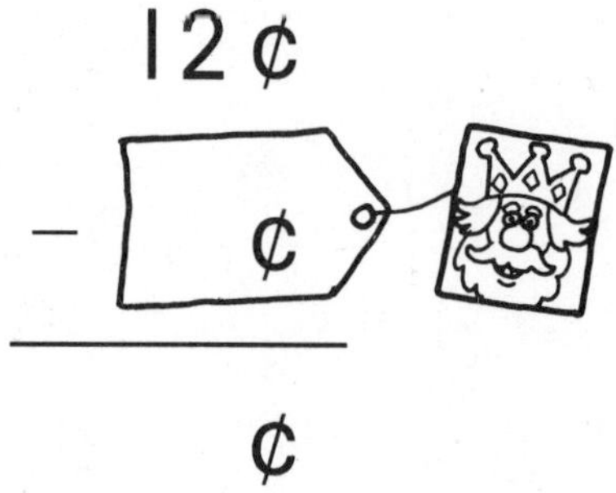

Number Sense

3. Who spent the same amount of money?

______________ and ______________

Use with text pages 257–258.

Name ____________________

8.12 USE WHAT YOU KNOW

Probability

Possible or Impossible

You need △ △ △ ○ □ [bag].

1. Put the shapes into the bag. Shake. Pick one.

   Color a □ to show your pick.

2. Make a prediction. If you pick 9 more times, which shape do you think you will pick most often?

   Ring your prediction. △ ○ □

3. Put the shape back into the bag. Shake. Repeat 9 more times.

△										
○										
□										
	0	1	2	3	4	5	6	7	8	9 10

4. Was your prediction right? Ring **Yes** or **No**.

   Yes No

Visual Thinking

5. Ring the shape you picked least often. △ ○ □

Name ______________________________

8.13
USE WHAT YOU KNOW

Problem Solving

Choose the Operation

Ring **Add** or **Subtract**.
Then write the number sentence.

1. Humpty Dumpty fell.
   9 men came.
   Then 3 more came.
   How many men came in all?

   9 (+) 3 = 12

Add   Subtract   12 men

2. Little Boy Blue has 9 sheep.
   He has 5 cows.
   How many more sheep than cows does he have?

   ____ ◯ ____ = ____

Add   Subtract   ____ more sheep

3. Little Bo-Peep had 11 sheep.
   She lost 3.
   How many sheep does she have left?

   ____ ◯ ____ = ____

Add   Subtract   ____ sheep

Story Corner

4. Make up an addition or a subtraction story about the picture.
   Draw a picture to show the story.

Use with text pages 261–262.

Name ____________________

9.1 USE WHAT YOU KNOW

Estimating and Comparing Length

You need crayons.

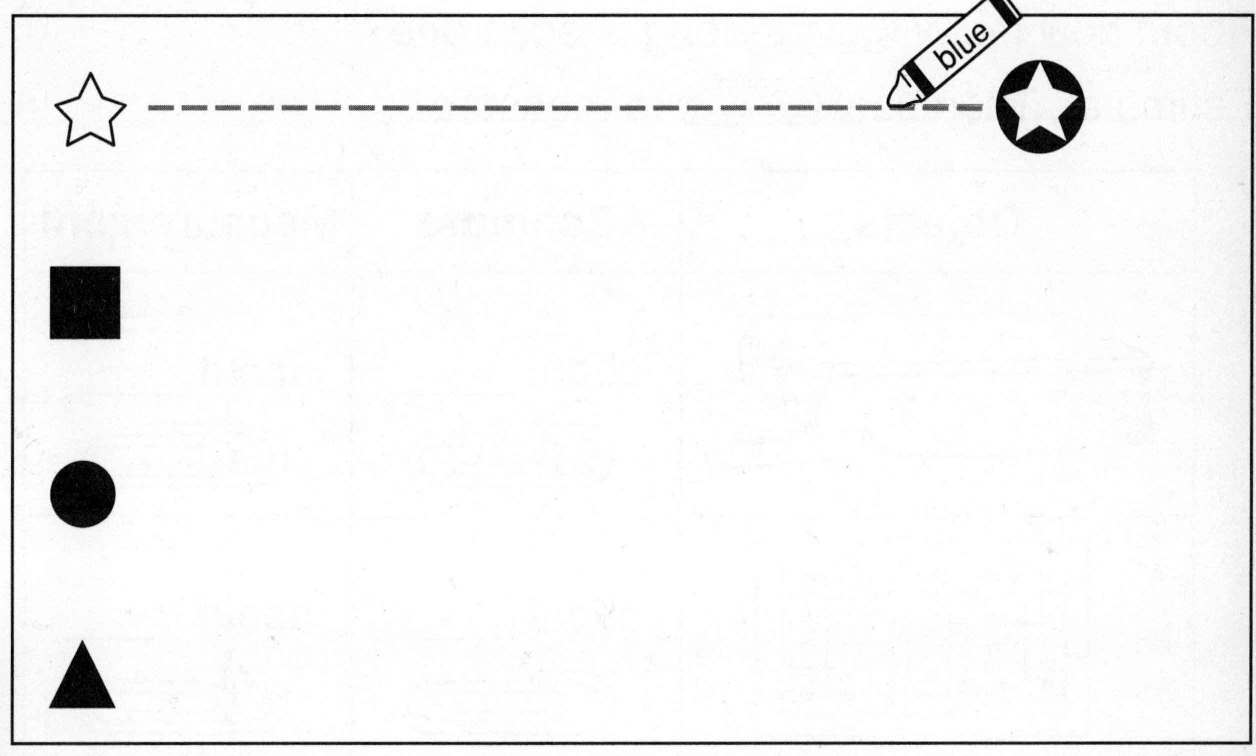

1. Start at ☆. Draw a blue line to the ✪.
2. Start at ■. Draw a yellow line that is as long as the blue line.
3. Start at ●. Draw a red line that is longer than the blue line.
4. Start at ▲. Draw a green line that is shorter than the blue line.

Visual Thinking

5. Cross out the object that is longer than the pencil.

Name ____________________

9.2 USE WHAT YOU KNOW

Measuring in Nonstandard Units

Find these objects in your classroom.

About how many (paper clips) long is each one?

Estimate. Then use (paper clips) to measure.

	Objects	Estimate	Measurement
1.		about ____ (paper clips)	about ____ (paper clips)
2.	APRIL 1994	about ____ (paper clips)	about ____ (paper clips)
3.		about ____ (paper clips)	about ____ (paper clips)
4.		about ____ (paper clips)	about ____ (paper clips)

Reasoning

5. What if you used a (large paper clip) to measure the objects?
Would you use more (pencils) or more (paper clips)?
Ring the answer.

Use with text pages 273–274

Name ____

Measuring in Inches

Use your inch ruler to measure.
Write how many inches tall.

1\.

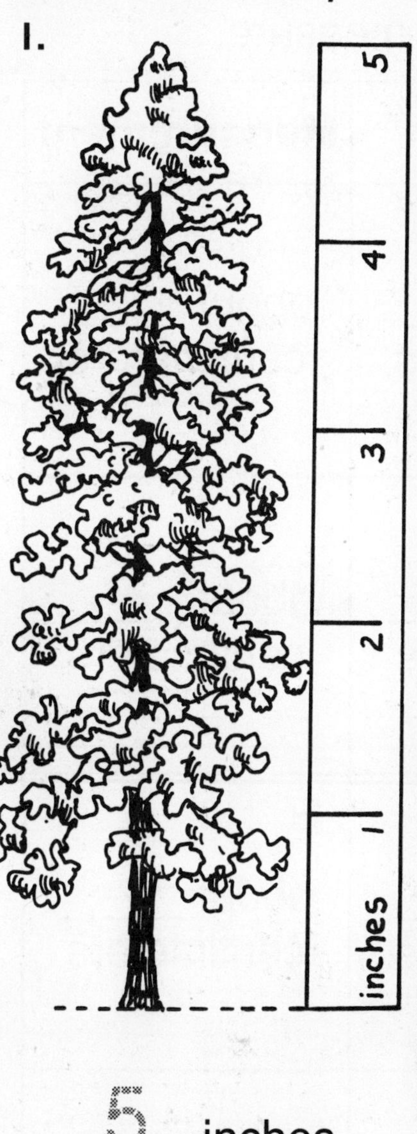

5 inches

2\.

______ inches

3\.

______ inches

4\.

______ inches

Reasoning

5\. What is the name of this shape.

6\. Measure the sides,
What did you find out?

Name ____

9.4 USE WHAT YOU KNOW

Measuring in Centimeters

Find these objects in your classroom.
About how many centimeters long is each one?
Estimate. Then use a centimeter ruler to measure.

	Objects	Estimate	Measurement
1.	chalk	about _____ centimeters	about _____ centimeters
2.	flag	about _____ centimeters	about _____ centimeters
3.	your lunchbox	about _____ centimeters	about _____ centimeters
4.	book	about _____ centimeters	about _____ centimeters

Number Sense

5. Ring in red the longest object.
6. Ring in blue the shortest object.

Use with text pages 277–278.

Name ____

9.5 USE WHAT YOU KNOW

More Measurement

Make a ruler.
Cut a strip of paper 10 centimeters long.

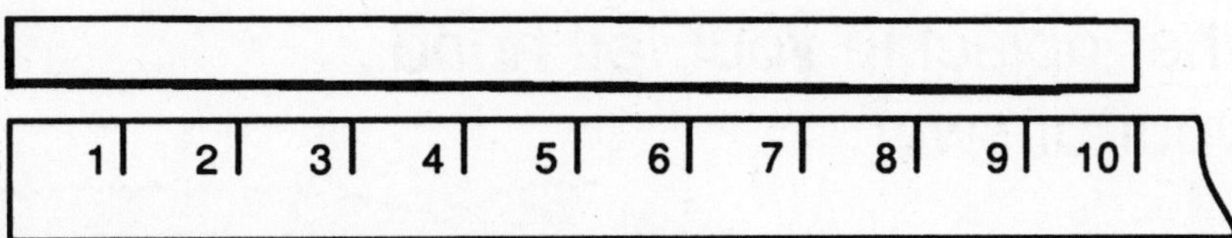

Draw an **X** to show your estimate.
Then use your ruler to check.
Draw a ✓ to show your measurement.

Objects	More than 10 centimeters	Less than 10 centimeters	About 10 centimeters
1. your arm	X ✓		
2. your shoe			
3. clock			
4. eraser			

Reasoning

5. 1 decimeter = 10 centimeters,

so 2 decimeters = _____ centimeters.

Use with text pages 279–280.

Name ___________________________________

9.6 USE WHAT YOU KNOW

Estimating and Measuring Weight

Which object in each pair is heavier?
Hold one object in your right hand.
Hold the other object in your left hand.
Then ring your answer.

1.

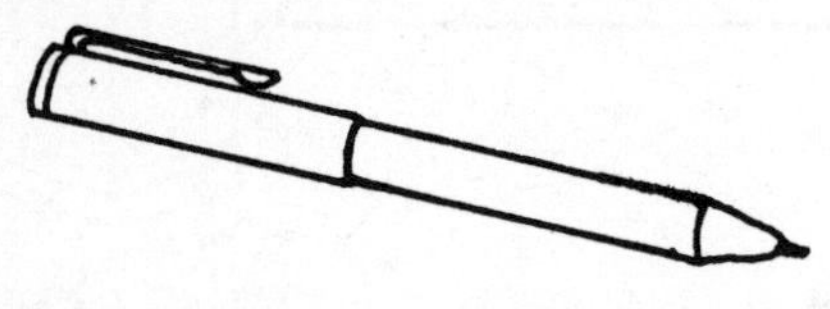

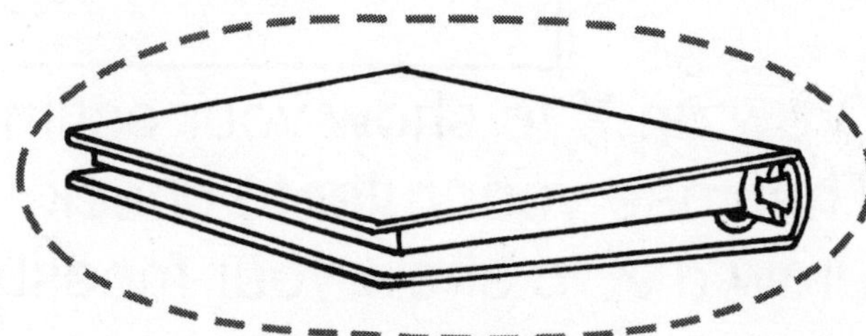

2.

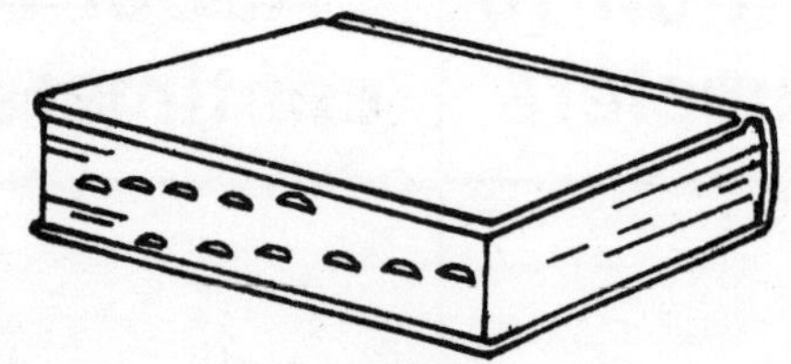

3.

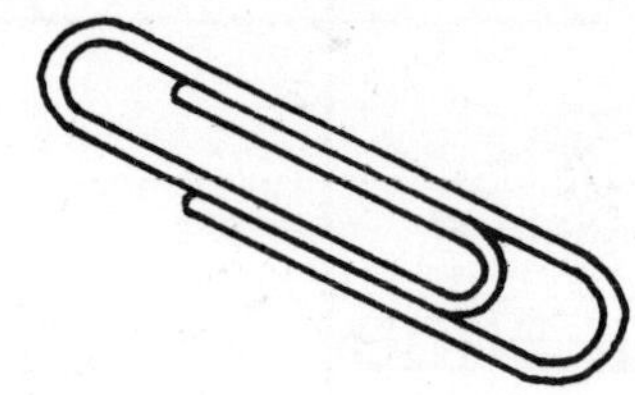

4.

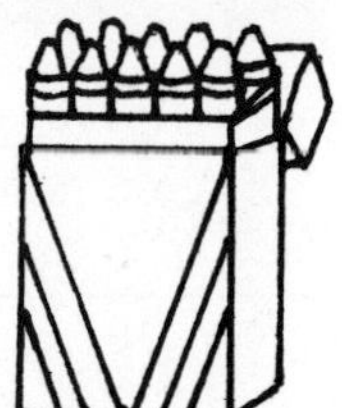

Reasoning

5. Ring the heaviest object.

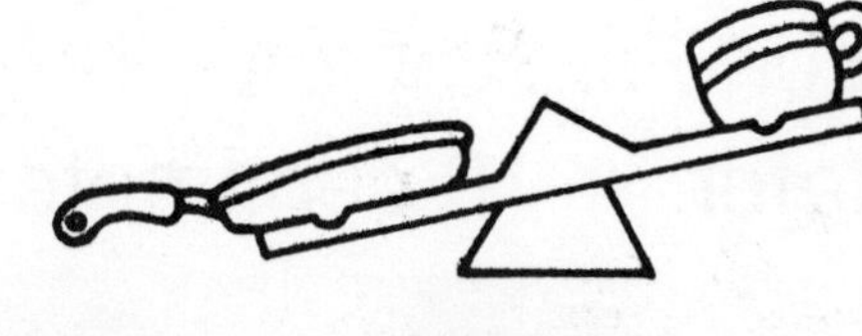

cup pan block

Use with text pages 281–282.

Name ______________________________

9.7
USE WHAT YOU KNOW

Estimating Capacity

About how many lids full of rice does each container hold?
You need these.

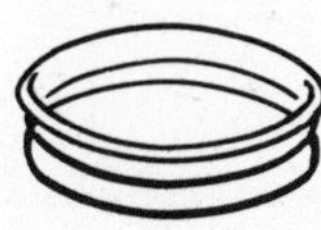
lid

rice

cup

milk carton

bowl

milk carton

Estimate. Then measure.

	Object	Estimate	Measurement
1.	cup	about _____ lids	about _____ lids
2.	milk carton	about _____ lids	about _____ lids
3.	bowl	about _____ lids	about _____ lids
4.	milk carton	about _____ lids	about _____ lids

Reasoning

5. Ring the one that holds more.

Name ____________________

Estimating Temperature

Which one in each pair is hot?
Ring it.

1.

2.

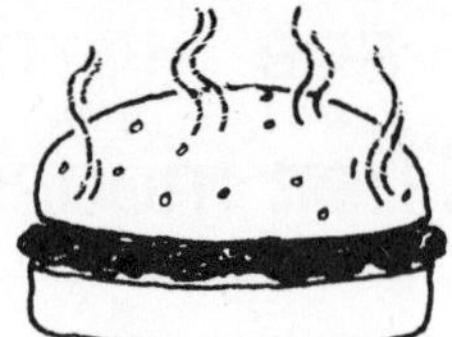

3.

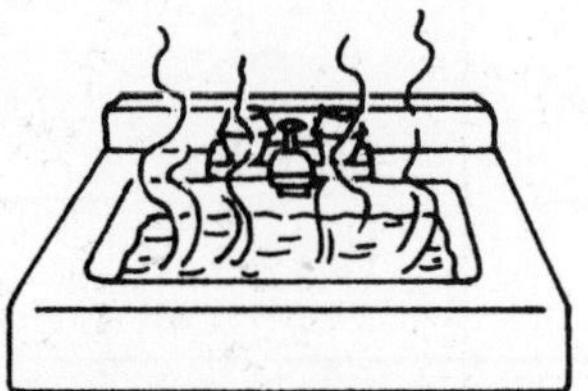

4.

Number Sense

Read the thermometers.

5. Ring the one that shows the hottest temperature.

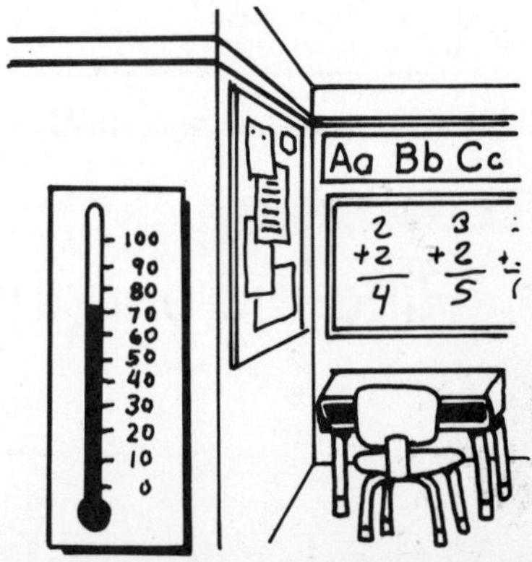

Use with text pages 285–286.

Name ______________________________

9.9

USE WHAT YOU KNOW

Problem Solving

Write Appropriate Questions

Some children counted birds they saw at a feeder. Then they made this table.

Birds at the Feeder			
Children	**First Week**	**Second Week**	**Third Week**
Joey	6	4	3
Laura	4	4	2
Khalid	5	2	4

1. Read the table. Write a question about the table.

____

____

Story Corner

2. Write another question about the table. Have your friend give the answer.

Name ______________________________

9.10

USE WHAT YOU KNOW

Fair Shares

Ring the ones that show fair shares.

1.

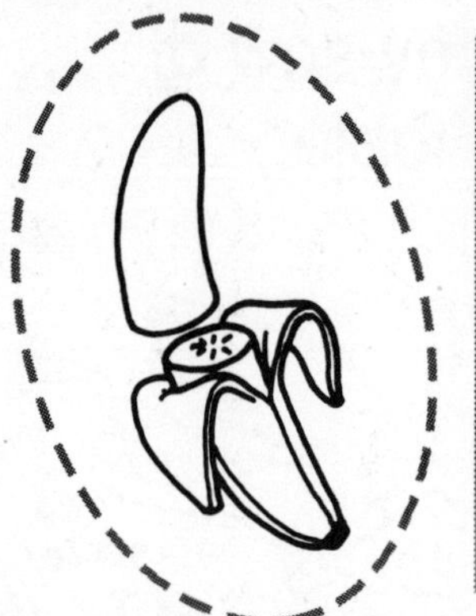

2.

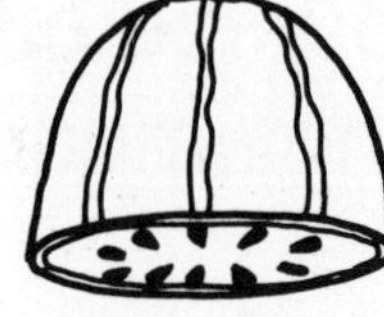

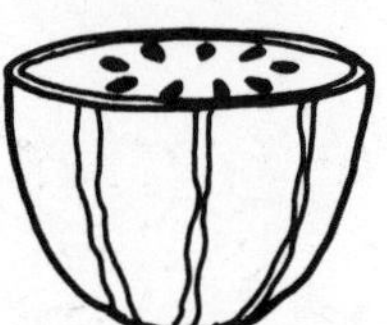

3.

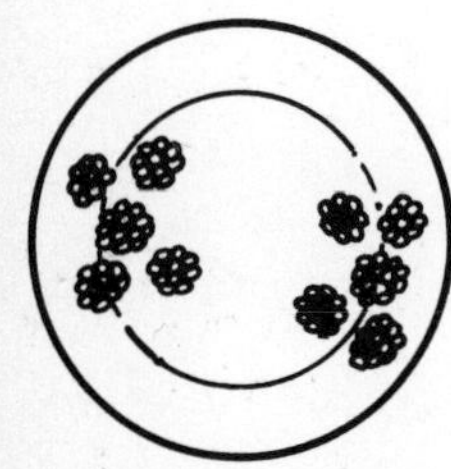

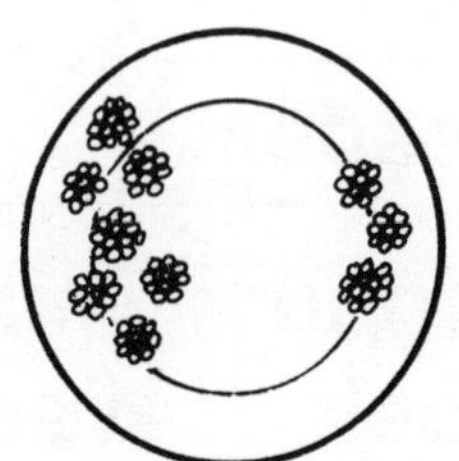

4.

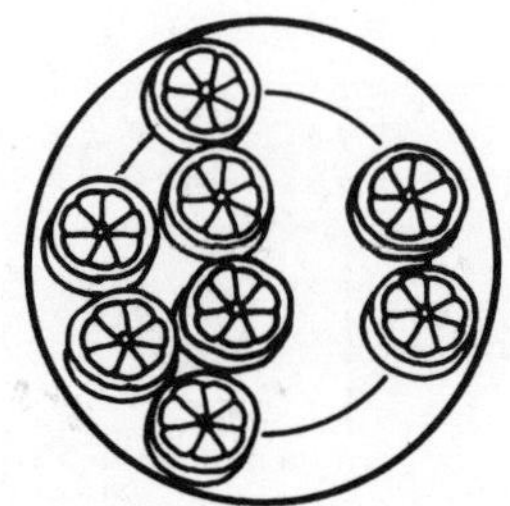

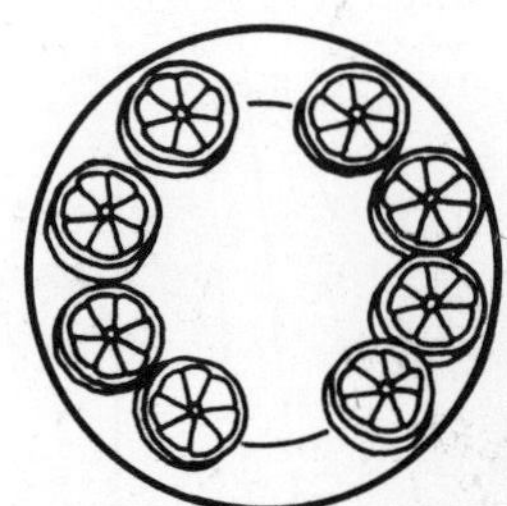

5.

6.

Visual Thinking

7. Rosa and Joey want fair shares of pizza.
How should the pizza be cut?
Draw a line to show.
Your pizza should show equal parts.

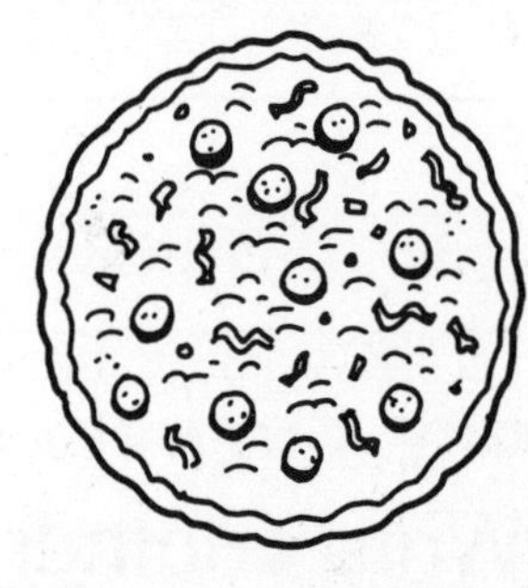

Use with text pages 291–292.

Name ______________________________

9.11
USE WHAT YOU KNOW

Halves

Draw a line to show two equal parts. Then color to show $\frac{1}{2}$.

1. 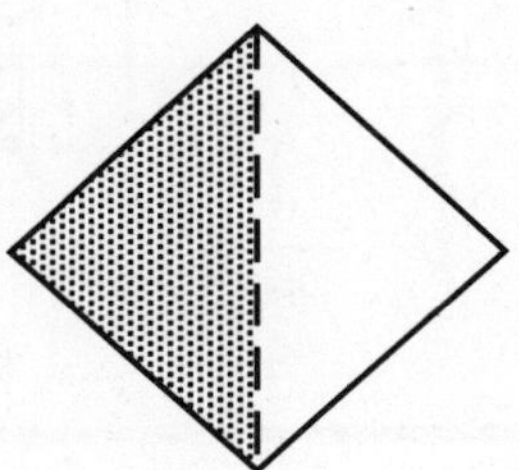

2. 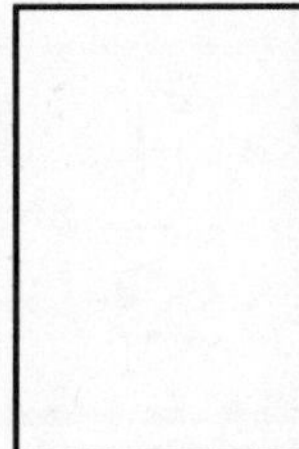

3. 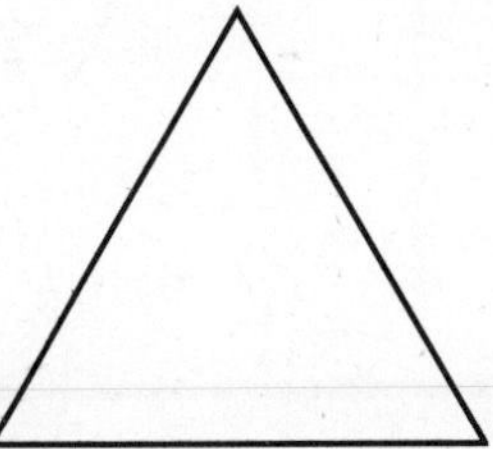

4. 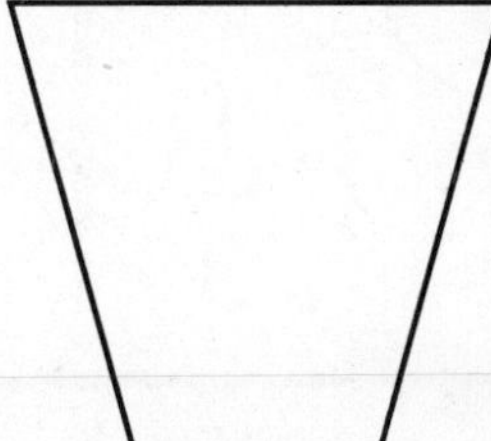

Find the shapes that show two equal parts. Color $\frac{1}{2}$.

5. 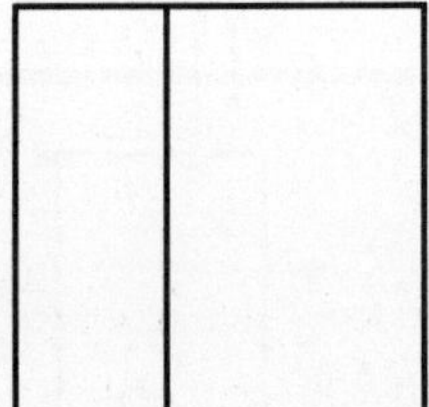 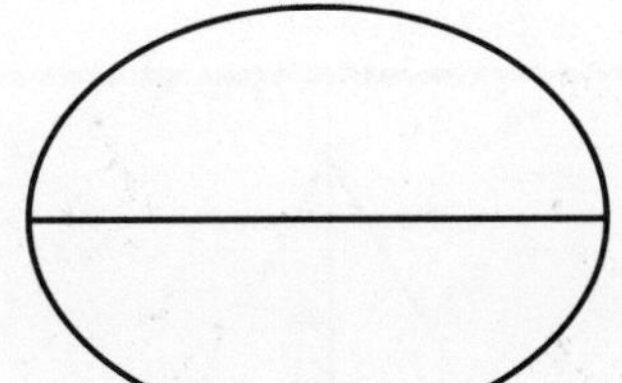 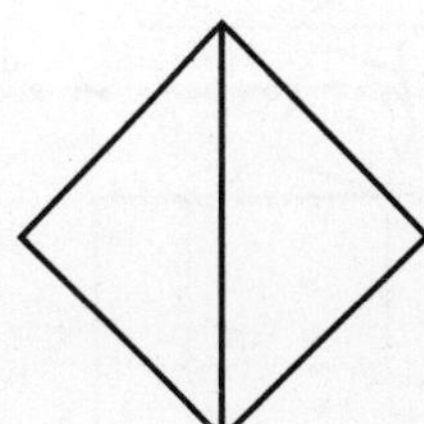

Problem Solving

Solve.

6. Two squirrels shared 4 nuts.
Each had one half of the 4 nuts.
How many nuts did each squirrel have?

_____ nuts

Name ______________________________

9.12

USE WHAT YOU KNOW

Thirds

Ring the fraction that each shape shows.

1.

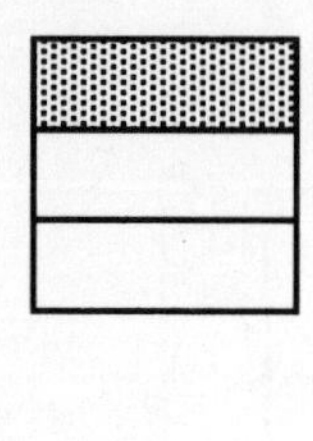

$\frac{1}{2}$ $\frac{1}{3}$

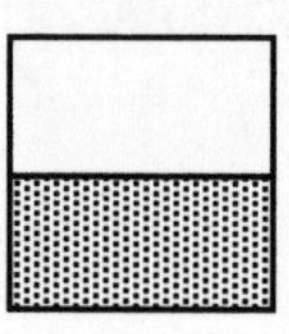

$\frac{1}{2}$ $\frac{1}{3}$

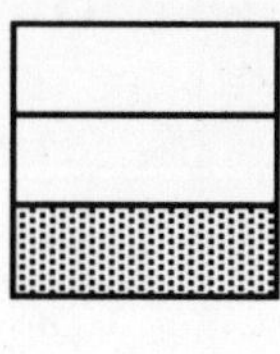

$\frac{1}{2}$ $\frac{1}{3}$

2.

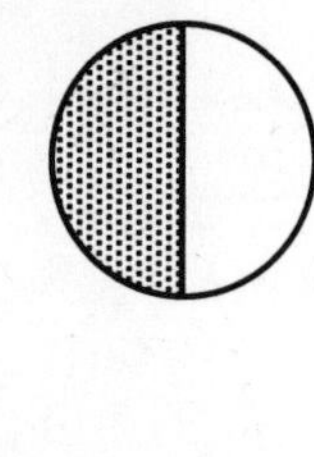

$\frac{1}{2}$ $\frac{1}{3}$

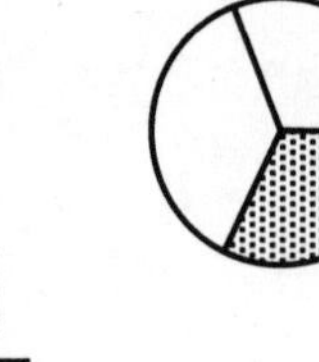

$\frac{1}{2}$ $\frac{1}{3}$

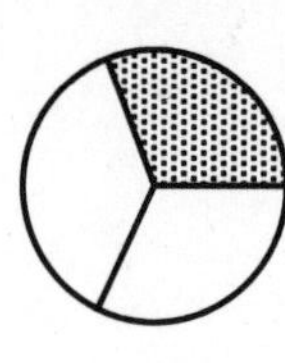

$\frac{1}{2}$ $\frac{1}{3}$

Find the shapes that show three equal parts. Color $\frac{1}{3}$.

3.

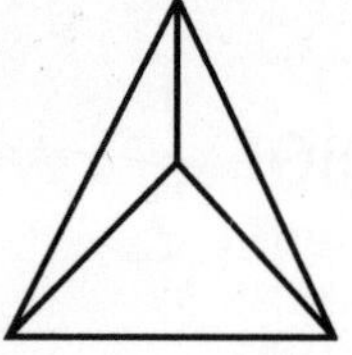

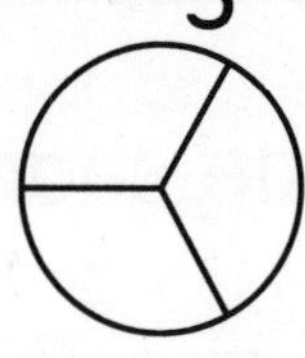

4.

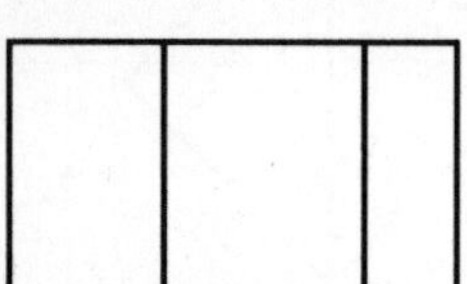

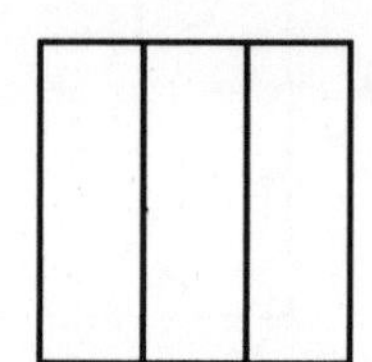

Visual Thinking

5. Which is greater, $\frac{1}{2}$ or $\frac{1}{3}$?

Ring the greater fraction.

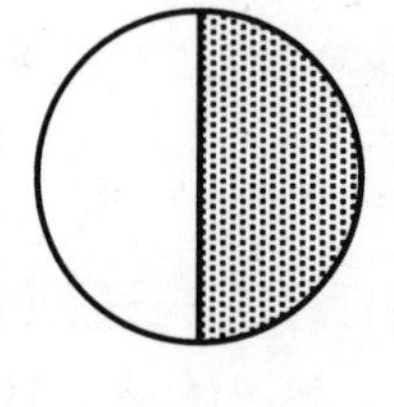

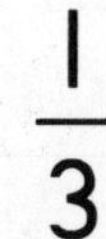

$\frac{1}{2}$ $\frac{1}{3}$

Use with text pages 295–296.

Name ____________________

Fourths

Ring the fraction that each shape shows.

1.

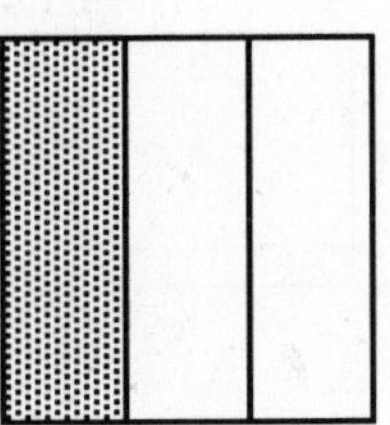

$\frac{1}{2}$ $\frac{1}{3}$ $\frac{1}{4}$

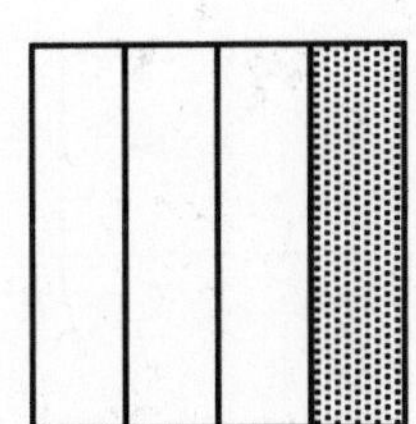

$\frac{1}{2}$ $\frac{1}{3}$ $\frac{1}{4}$

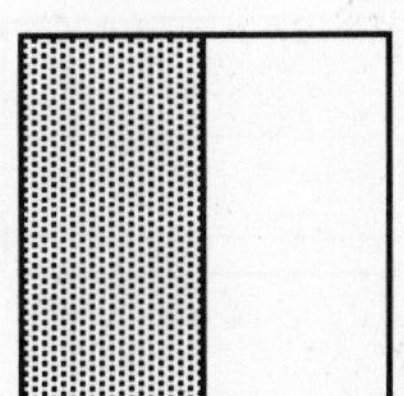

$\frac{1}{2}$ $\frac{1}{3}$ $\frac{1}{4}$

2.

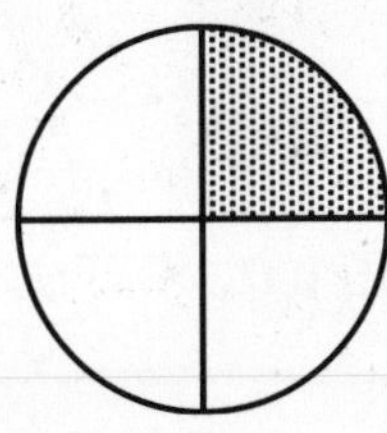

$\frac{1}{2}$ $\frac{1}{3}$ $\frac{1}{4}$

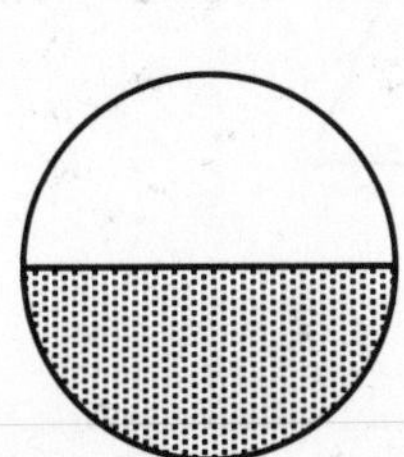

$\frac{1}{2}$ $\frac{1}{3}$ $\frac{1}{4}$

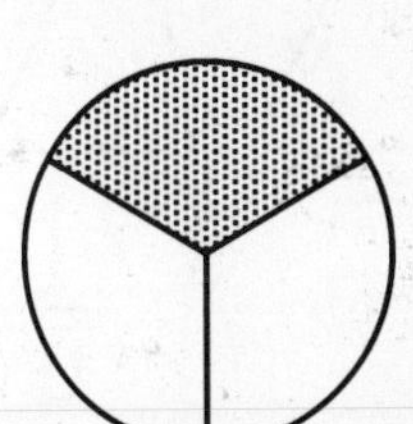

$\frac{1}{2}$ $\frac{1}{3}$ $\frac{1}{4}$

Find the shapes that show four equal parts. Color $\frac{1}{4}$.

3.

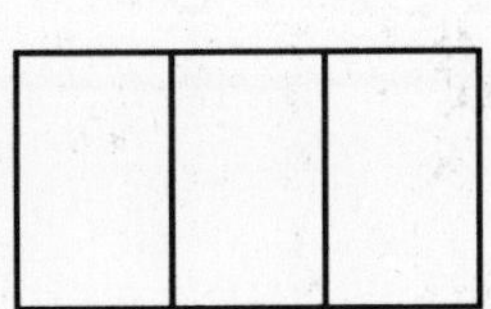

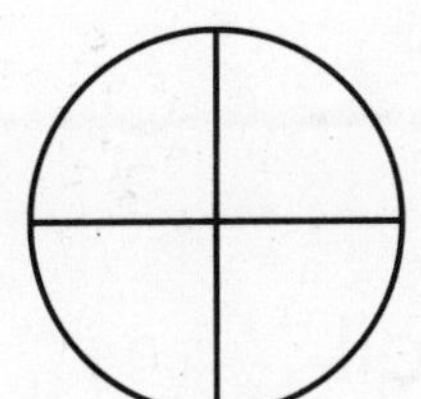

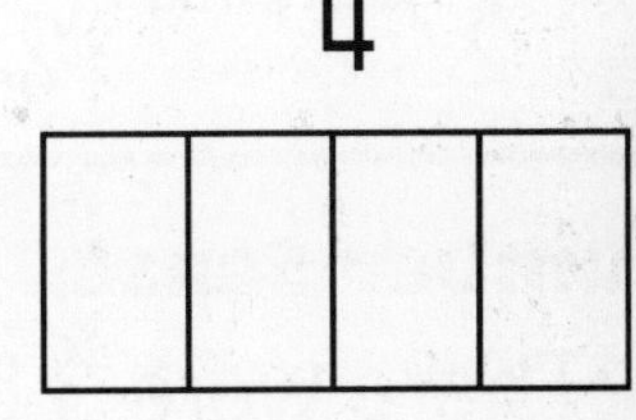

Visual Thinking

4. Which is greater, $\frac{1}{3}$ or $\frac{1}{4}$?

Ring the greater fraction.

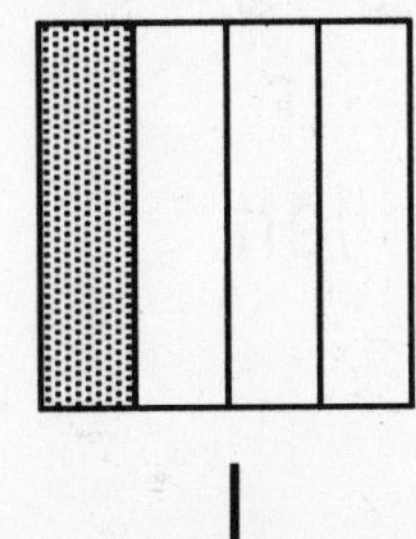

$\frac{1}{4}$

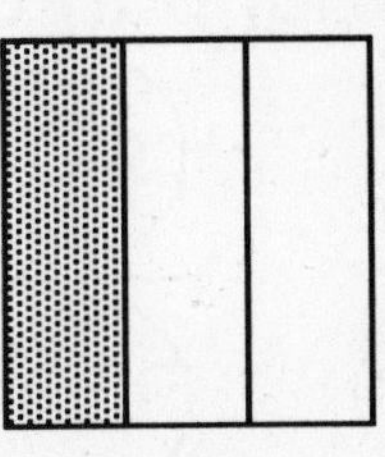

$\frac{1}{3}$

Name ______________________________

Fractions in Groups

Color to show each fraction

1. 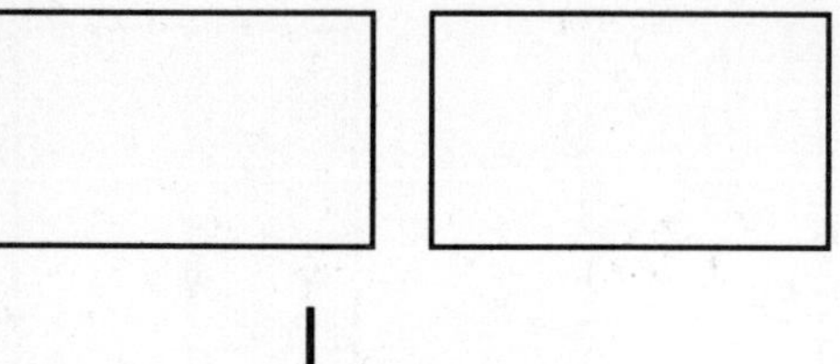

$\frac{1}{2}$ blue

2. 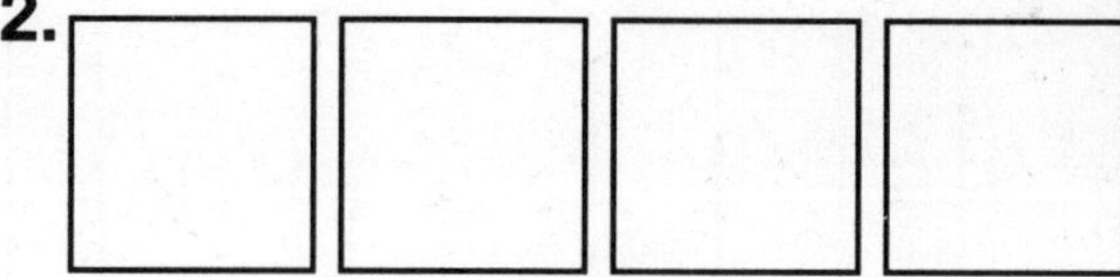

$\frac{1}{4}$ green

3. 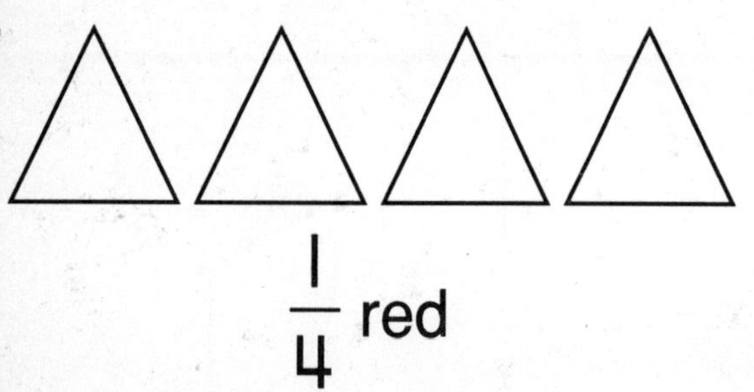

$\frac{1}{4}$ red

4. 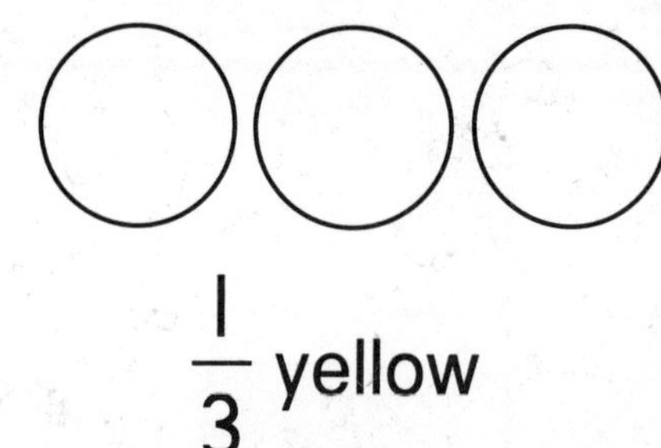

$\frac{1}{3}$ yellow

5. 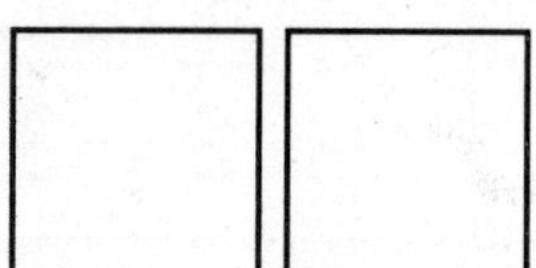

$\frac{1}{2}$ purple, $\frac{1}{2}$ orange

6. 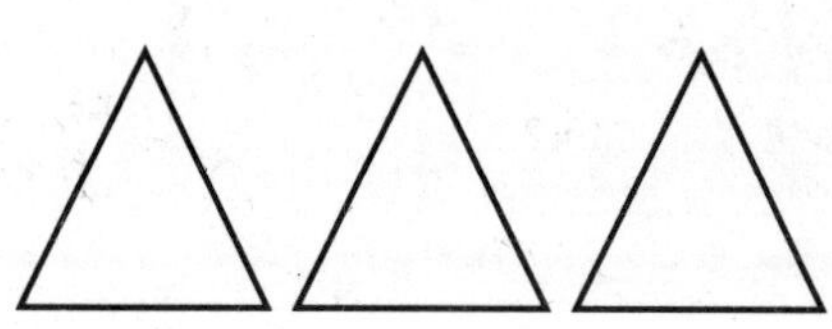

$\frac{1}{3}$ green, $\frac{1}{3}$ red, $\frac{1}{3}$ blue

Number Sense

7. There were 3 bears in all.
Write the fraction that tells what part of the group is left.

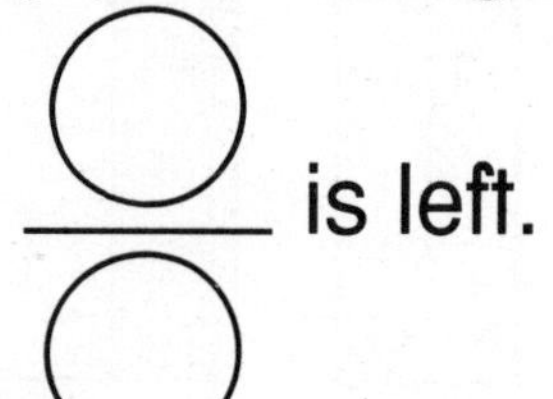

is left.

Use with text pages 299–300.

Name ____

9.15
USE WHAT YOU KNOW

Problem Solving

Visualize the Results

What is missing from each circle on the right?
Find the missing part. Draw lines to match.

1. $\frac{1}{2}$ 

2. $\frac{1}{3}$ 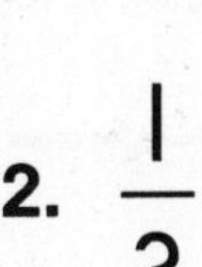 

3. $\frac{1}{4}$ 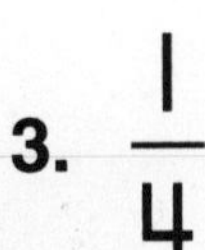 

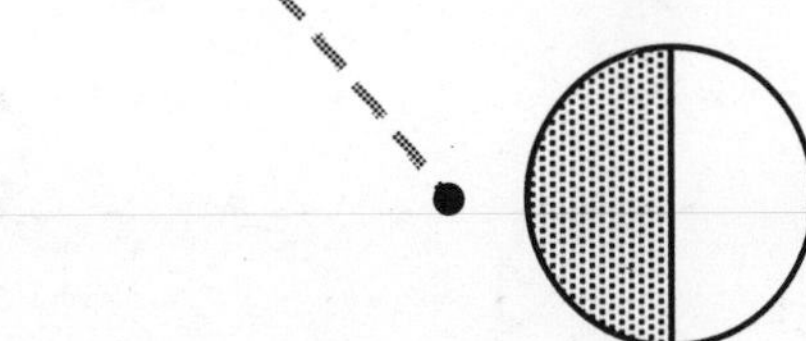

How does the rest of each picture look?
Draw the missing part to complete.

4. 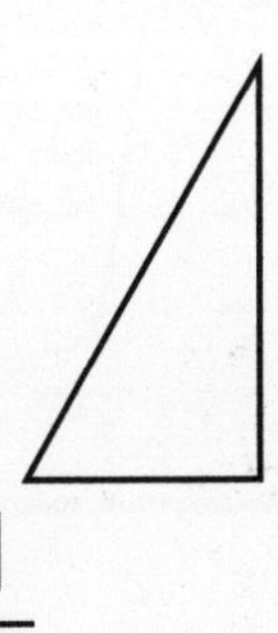

$\frac{1}{2}$ a triangle

5. 

$\frac{1}{3}$ a pie

Number Sense

6. There were 3 fair shares.
Ring the fraction that tells what part of the pizza has been eaten.

$\frac{1}{2}$ $\frac{2}{3}$

Name ____________________

10.1

USE WHAT YOU KNOW

Ordering Events

Ring in green what happened first.
Ring in red what happened last.

1.

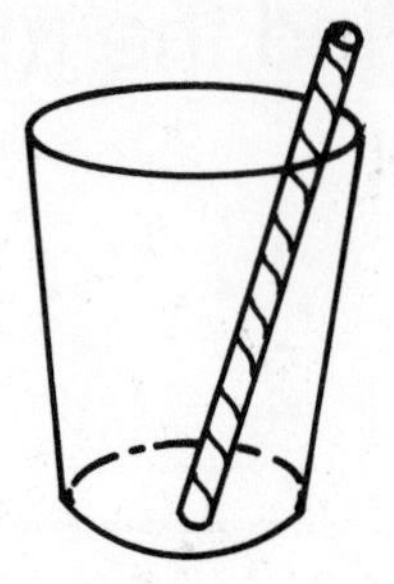

2.

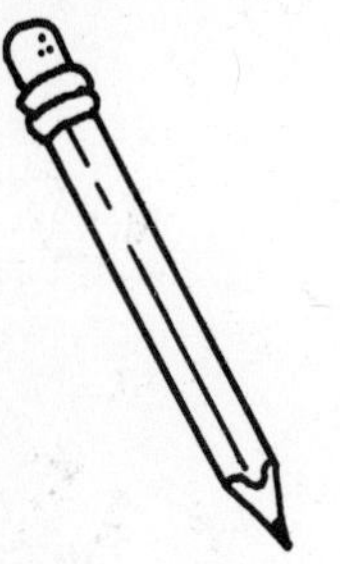

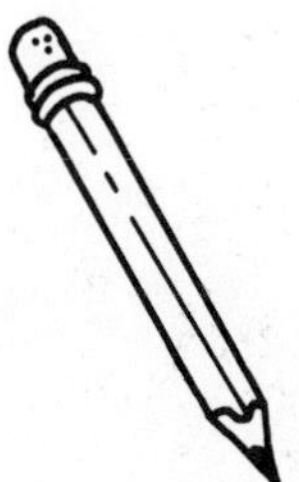

3.

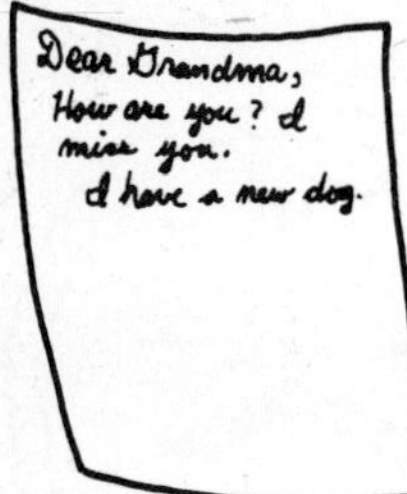

Dear Grandma,
How are you? I miss you.
I have a new dog.
My dog's name is Spot. He is a little dog.
He sleeps in my room.
Mom said that we will come to see you soon.
Love,
Carol

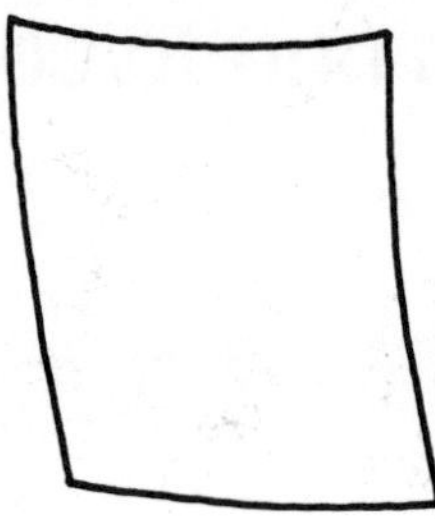

Dear Grandma,
How are you? I miss you.
I have a new dog.
My dog's name is Spot. He is a little dog.
He sleeps in my room.

Story Corner

4. Make up a story about the pictures.
Share your story with a friend.

Use with text pages 313–314.

Name ____________________

Estimating Time

Which takes more time to complete? Ring it.

1.

2.

Which takes less time? Ring it.

3.

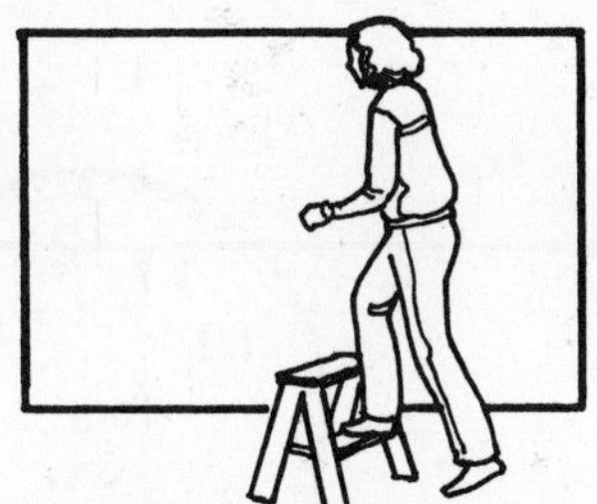

4.

Number Sense

5. Which takes the most time? Ring it.

Use with text pages 315–316.

Name ______________________________

10.3 USE WHAT YOU KNOW

Reading the Clock

Show each time on your .
Trace the hour hand on each clock.
Write the time.

1.

3 o'clock

2.

_____ o'clock

3.

_____ o'clock

Show each time on your  .
Trace the minute hand on each clock.
Write the time.

4.

_____ o'clock

5.

_____ o'clock

6.

_____ o'clock

Problem Solving

Use your  .

7. Travis's clock showed 4 o'clock.
Lee moved the short hand to the next hour.
Then Nell moved the short hand to the next hour.
What time does the clock show now?

_____ o'clock

Use with text pages 317–318.

Name ______________________________

10.4
USE WHAT YOU KNOW

Hour

Draw the hour hand so that both clocks show the same time.

1.

11:00

Write the time on the clock so that both clocks show the same time.

2.

Number Sense

3. Write the time on the clock so that it shows 1 hour later than 11 o'clock.

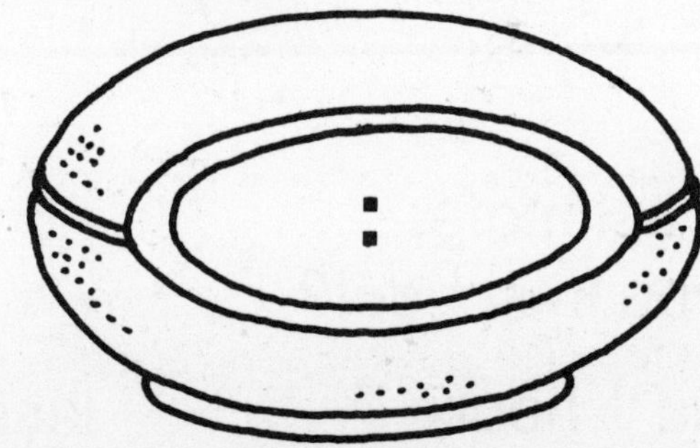

Name ____________________

10.5
USE WHAT YOU KNOW

Exploring Minutes

Work with a friend.

Ring in orange your estimates.

Use your  or ⌛ to time each other.

Ring in green to show how much time passed.

1. 

Write your name 1 time.

more than 1 minute

less than 1 minute

---

2. 

Tell a long story.

more than 1 minute

less than 1 minute

---

3. 

Count backward from 99 to 1.

more than 1 minute

less than 1 minute

Number Sense

4. Ring the better estimate.
How long are you in school?

more than 1 hour　　　　less than 1 hour

Use with text pages 321–322.

Name ____

Thirty Minutes

Write each time.

1.

8:00

:

:

2.

:

:

:

Show the time. Draw the minute hand.

3.

10:00

10:30

11:00

Number Sense

4. Ring the better estimate.
   How long will the movie last?

   more than 30 minutes

   less than 30 minutes

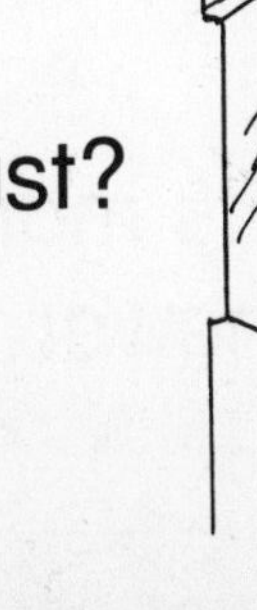

Use with text page 323–324.

Name ____________________

10.7 USE WHAT YOU KNOW

The Calendar

Complete the calendar for next month.

__________ , 19 ________

Sunday	Monday	Tuesday	Wednesday	Thursday	Friday	Saturday

Use the calendar. Write the answers.

1. How many days are in this month? __________ days
2. Name the first day of this month. __________
3. Name the last day of this month. __________
4. What day is today's date? __________

Number Sense

5. Look at calendars for this month and next month. Ring the answer.
   Next month is ? .

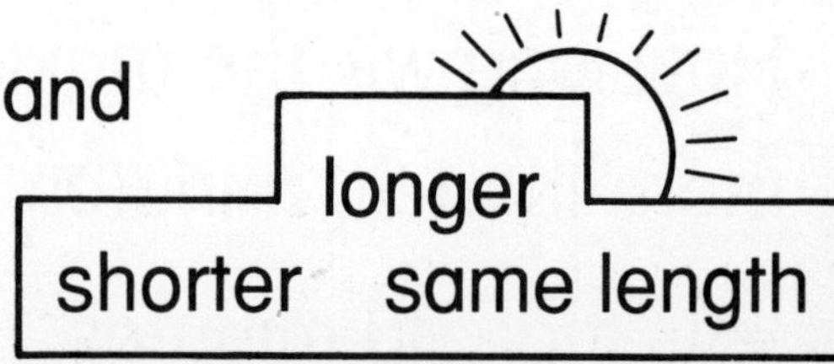

Use with text pages 325–326.

Name ____________________

10.8
USE WHAT YOU KNOW

Problem-Solving Strategy

Use a Model

Use your  to solve each problem.

Draw the hands on the clocks to show the times.

1. 

Brenda started her picture at 3:00. She finished 1 hour later. At what time did she finish?

2. 

George started eating lunch at 12:00. He finished 30 minutes later. At what time did he finish?

3. 

The music started at 8:00. It lasted 2 hours. At what time did it end?

Story Corner

4. Make up a story about the pictures. Share your story with a friend.

Name ______________________________ **10.9**

USE WHAT YOU KNOW

Penny and Nickel

Ring how much money is needed.

1.

2.

3.

Count by fives. Ring how much money is needed.

4.

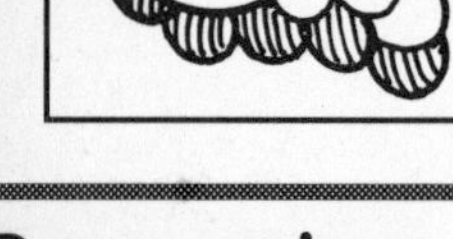

Reasoning

Ring the one that costs less.

5.

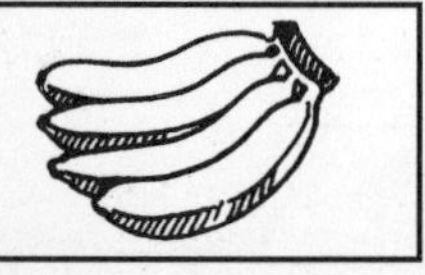
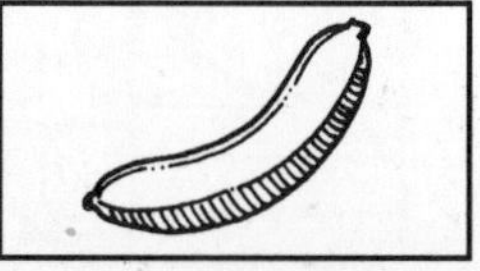

6.

Use with text pages 331–332.

Name ______________________________

10.10
USE WHAT YOU KNOW

Dime

Count by fives and tens.
Ring how much money is needed.

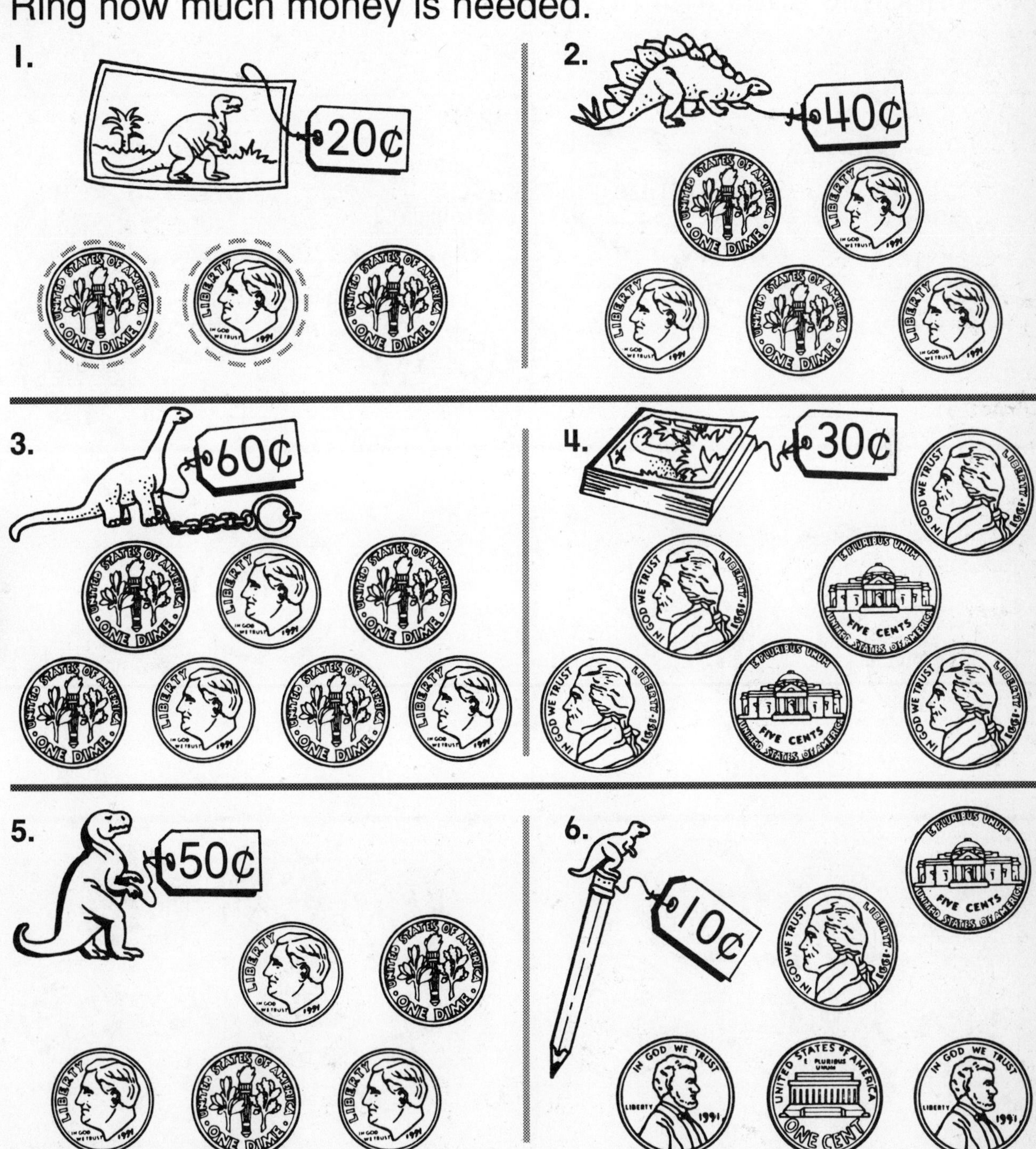

Number Sense

7. Ring the greatest amount.

20 pennies 4 dimes 5 nickels

Name ______________________________

10.11 USE WHAT YOU KNOW

Quarter

Write each amount.
Then ring the ones that have the same value as a (quarter).

1.

20 ¢

2.

_____ ¢

3.

_____ ¢

4.

_____ ¢

5.

_____ ¢

6.

_____ ¢

Reasoning

7. Ring the amount that you can show with the least number of coins. 15¢ 20¢ 25¢

Use with text pages 335–336.

Name ____________________

Counting On from Nickels and Dimes

How much money? Count on.
Write the amount. Use punch-out coins.

1.

10 ¢ 20 ¢ 30 ¢ 31 ¢ 32 ¢ 32 ¢

2.

____ ¢ ____ ¢ ____ ¢ ____ ¢ ____ ¢ ☐ ¢

Write the amount.

3.

____ ¢

4.

____ ¢

Number Sense

5. Ring the greater amount.

2 dimes 9 pennies   4 nickels 8 pennies

Name ______________________________

10.13
USE WHAT YOU KNOW

Counting On from a Quarter

How much money? Count on from 25¢.
Write the amount. Use punch-out coins.

1.        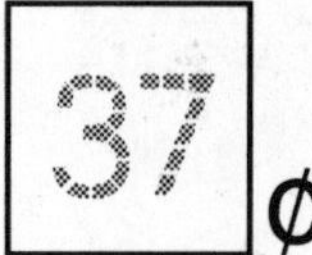

25 ¢ 30 ¢ 35 ¢ 36 ¢ 37 ¢ [37] ¢

2.      

____ ¢ ____ ¢ ____ ¢ ____ ¢ [ ] ¢

3.      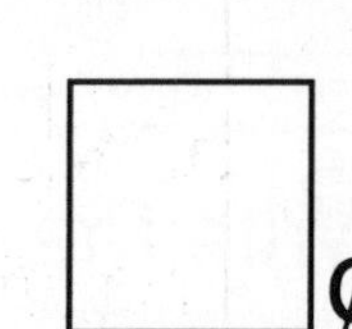

____ ¢ ____ ¢ ____ ¢ ____ ¢ ____ ¢ [ ] ¢

4.       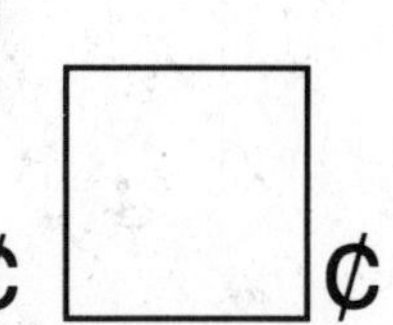

____ ¢ ____ ¢ ____ ¢ ____ ¢ ____ ¢ ____ ¢ [ ] ¢

Number Sense

5. Ring the coins to make 50¢.

Use with text pages 339–340.

Name ____________________

10.14 USE WHAT YOU KNOW

Equal Amounts

Use your punch-out coins. Show a different way to make the same amount. Draw the coins you used. Write the value on each coin.

1.

2.

Use a  to find each amount. Match equal amounts.

3.

4.

Number Sense

5. Ring **Yes** or **No**. Can you show 20¢ with 3 coins? Yes No

Name ________________________

10.15
USE WHAT YOU KNOW

Problem-Solving Strategy

Make a Model

Solve each problem. Act it out with a friend. Use punch-out coins. Write the amount.

1. Robert has 2 nickels and 4 dimes. He trades the 2 nickels for 1 dime. How much money does Robert have?

   50 ¢

2. Sharon has 2 dimes and 10 pennies. She trades the 10 pennies for 1 dime. How much money does Sharon have?

   _____ ¢

3. Hannah has 5 nickels and 2 dimes. She trades 4 nickels for 2 dimes. How much money does Hannah have?

   _____ ¢

4. Roy has 3 dimes, 2 nickels, and 2 pennies. He trades 2 dimes and 1 nickel for 1 quarter. How much money does Roy have?

   _____ ¢

Reasoning

5. You want to have fewer coins. Ring the coins you would give and take in a trade.

Give	Take
dime dime dime dime	quarter quarter dime
dime nickel nickel nickel	nickel penny penny
	penny penny penny

Use with text pages 343–344.

Name ______________________________

11.1 USE WHAT YOU KNOW

Adding and Subtracting

Do these in your head. Complete each table. Look for a pattern.

1.

Add 2.	
7	9
8	
9	
10	

2.

Subtract 2.	
7	
8	
9	
10	

Match the pairs that have the same sum.

3.

2 + 6 •	• 7 + 3
3 + 7 •	• 5 + 2
2 + 5 •	• 6 + 2

4.

0 + 8 •	• 6 + 3
2 + 8 •	• 8 + 0
3 + 6 •	• 8 + 2

Reasoning

Ring the answer.

5. Since 8 + 3 = 11,
then 7 + ? = 11.

4 5 6

6. Since 8 + 4 = 12,
then 7 + ? = 12.

3 4 5

Name ____________________

11.2
USE WHAT YOU KNOW

Tens and Ones

Ring groups of ten.
Write how many stars in all.

1.

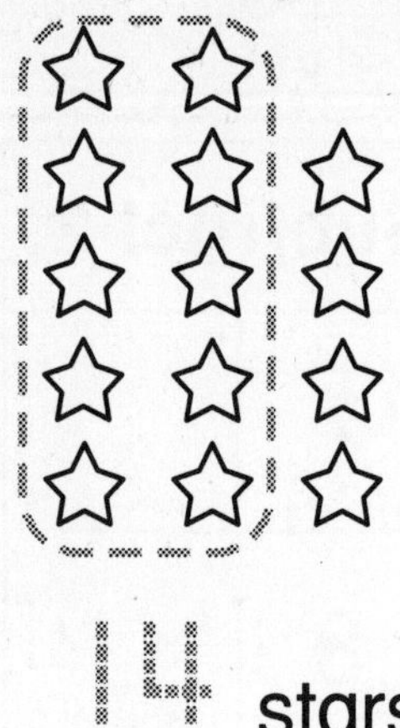

14 stars

2.

_____ stars

3.

_____ stars

4.

_____ stars

Number Sense • Estimation

About how many strawberries are in each bag?
Ring the better estimate.

60 Strawberries

5.

more than 30

fewer than 30

6.

between 40 and 60

between 10 and 30

Use with text pages 355–356.

Name ____

11.3
USE WHAT YOU KNOW

Adding Tens

Add tens. Write each addition sentence.

1. 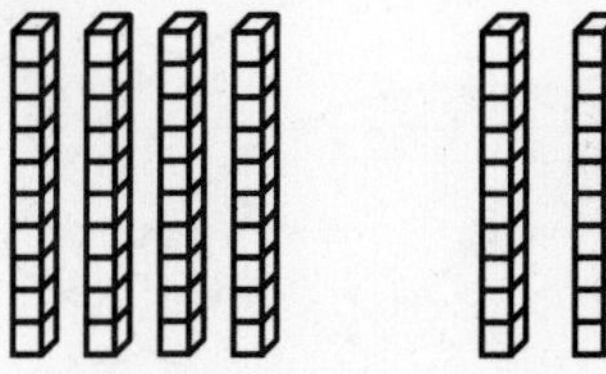

40 + 20 = 60

2.  

_____ + _____ = _____

3. 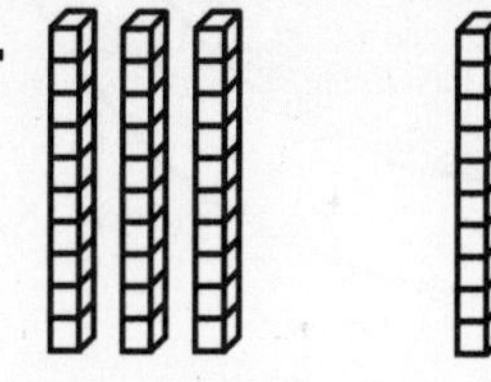

_____ + _____ = _____

4. 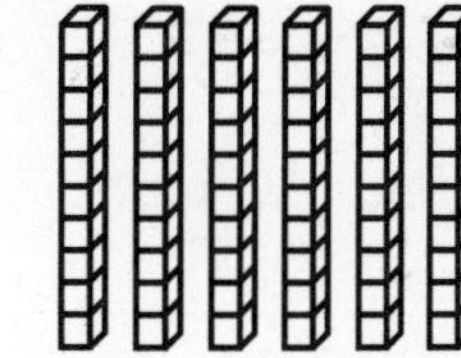 

_____ + _____ = _____

5. 

_____ + _____ = _____

6. 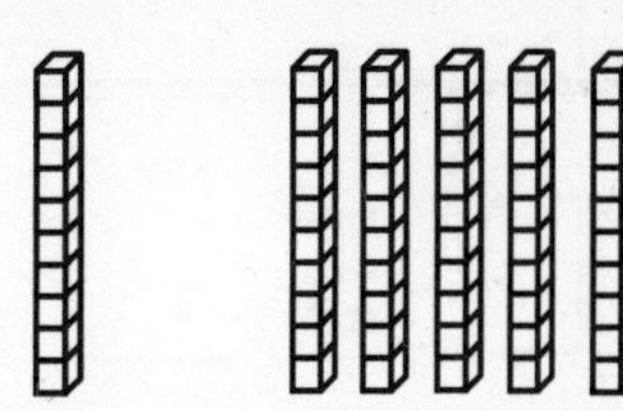

_____ + _____ = _____

Number Sense

Do these in your head. Match the pairs to their sums.

7.

7 + 1 •	• 30
20 + 10 •	• 6
2 + 4 •	• 8

8.

40 + 30 •	• 40
20 + 20 •	• 9
5 + 4 •	• 70

Name ______________________________

Exploring 2-Digit Addition

Use a pencil and a paper clip to make a spinner.
Spin the paper clip.
Write the number in the box.
Add. Write the sum.
Use punch-out tens and ones if you need to.

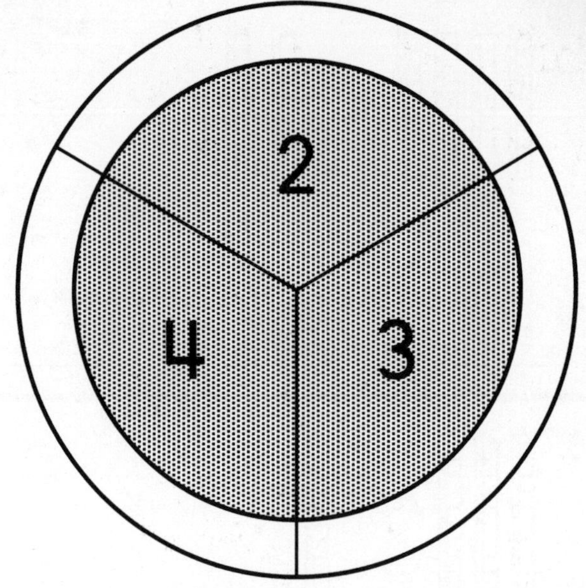

1. 54 + [3] = 57
2. 91 + [ ] = ____
3. 65 + [ ] = ____
4. 32 + [ ] = ____
5. 73 + [ ] = ____
6. 40 + [ ] = ____
7. 81 + [ ] = ____
8. 24 + [ ] = ____
9. 50 + [ ] = ____
10. 62 + [ ] = ____

Story Corner

Solve the riddle.

11. I am 1 more than 3 tens and 6 ones.
What number am I?
____

12. I am 2 more than 4 tens and 5 ones.
What number am I?
____

Use with text pages 359–360.

Name ____________________

11.5 USE WHAT YOU KNOW

Adding 2-Digit Numbers

Use punch-out tens and ones and Workmat 3. Add.

1.

tens	ones
5	8
+ 1	1
6	9

tens	ones
2	5
+ 2	3

tens	ones
4	3
+	2

tens	ones
1	2
+ 7	5

2. $66 + 13$ $\quad 32 + 4$ $\quad 71 + 24$ $\quad 27 + 60$ $\quad 54 + 43$

Number Sense

Solve the first problem. Then ring the better estimate for each problem. Use tens and ones models to check your estimate.

3. $40 + 40$

$40 + 51$
more than 80
less than 80

$36 + 32$
more than 80
less than 80

4. $10 + 10$

$15 + 2$
more than 20
less than 20

$23 + 14$
more than 20
less than 20

Name ______________________________

11.6

USE WHAT YOU KNOW

Subtracting Tens

Use punch-out tens and ones and Workmat 3. Add or subtract.

1.	70	50	80	60	40
	+ 10	+ 20	− 30	− 20	+ 30
	80				
2.	80	60	70	40	50
	− 20	− 40	+ 20	− 20	+ 40
3.	80	60	70	60	80
	+ 10	+ 30	− 40	− 30	− 10

Number Sense

Do these in your head. Look for a pattern.

4.	43	53	63	73	83
	+ 10	+ 10	+ 10	+ 10	+ 10
5.	43	53	63	73	83
	− 10	− 10	− 10	− 10	− 10

Use with text pages 365–366.

Name ______________________________

Exploring 2-Digit Subtraction

Use a pencil and a paper clip to make a spinner.
Spin the paper clip.
Write the number in the box.
Subtract.
Write how many are left.
Use punch-out tens and ones if you need to.

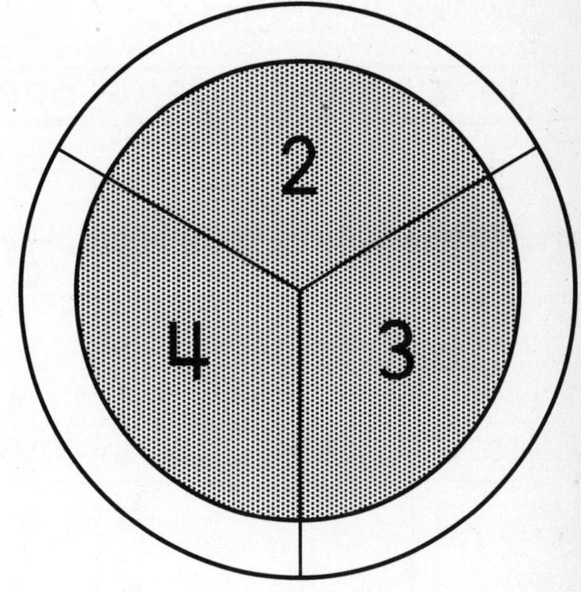

1. 45 − [4] = 41
2. 28 − [ ] = ____
3. 89 − [ ] = ____
4. 66 − [ ] = ____
5. 37 − [ ] = ____
6. 55 − [ ] = ____
7. 76 − [ ] = ____
8. 48 − [ ] = ____
9. 85 − [ ] = ____
10. 39 − [ ] = ____

Story Corner

Solve the riddle.

11. I am 1 less than 5 tens and 3 ones. What number am I?

____

12. I am 2 less than 6 tens and 7 ones. What number am I?

____

Name ______________________________

11.8
USE WHAT YOU KNOW

Subtracting 2-Digit Numbers

Use punch-out tens and ones and Workmat 3. Subtract.

1.

tens	ones
2	4
−	3
2	1

tens	ones
7	9
− 4	6

tens	ones
5	5
− 5	2

tens	ones
6	6
− 5	2

2.

tens	ones
4	8
− 2	6

tens	ones
8	9
− 4	2

tens	ones
3	5
− 1	3

tens	ones
2	7
− 1	4

3. $\begin{array}{r} 70 \\ -\ 30 \\ \hline \end{array}$ $\quad \begin{array}{r} 33 \\ -\ 12 \\ \hline \end{array}$ $\quad \begin{array}{r} 96 \\ -\ 33 \\ \hline \end{array}$ $\quad \begin{array}{r} 49 \\ -\ 35 \\ \hline \end{array}$ $\quad \begin{array}{r} 55 \\ -\ 23 \\ \hline \end{array}$

Number Sense

Solve the first problem. Then ring the better estimate for each problem. Use tens and ones models to check your estimate.

4. $\begin{array}{r} 60 \\ -\ 20 \\ \hline \end{array}$ $\quad \begin{array}{r} 60 \\ -\ 30 \\ \hline \end{array}$ $\quad \begin{array}{r} 60 \\ -\ 10 \\ \hline \end{array}$

60 − 30	60 − 10
more than 40	more than 40
less than 40	less than 40

Use with text pages 369–370.

Name ________________________________

11.9
USE WHAT YOU KNOW

Adding and Subtracting

Add or subtract.
Color.

20 to 30	40 to 50	60 to 70	80 to 90
red	yellow	blue	brown

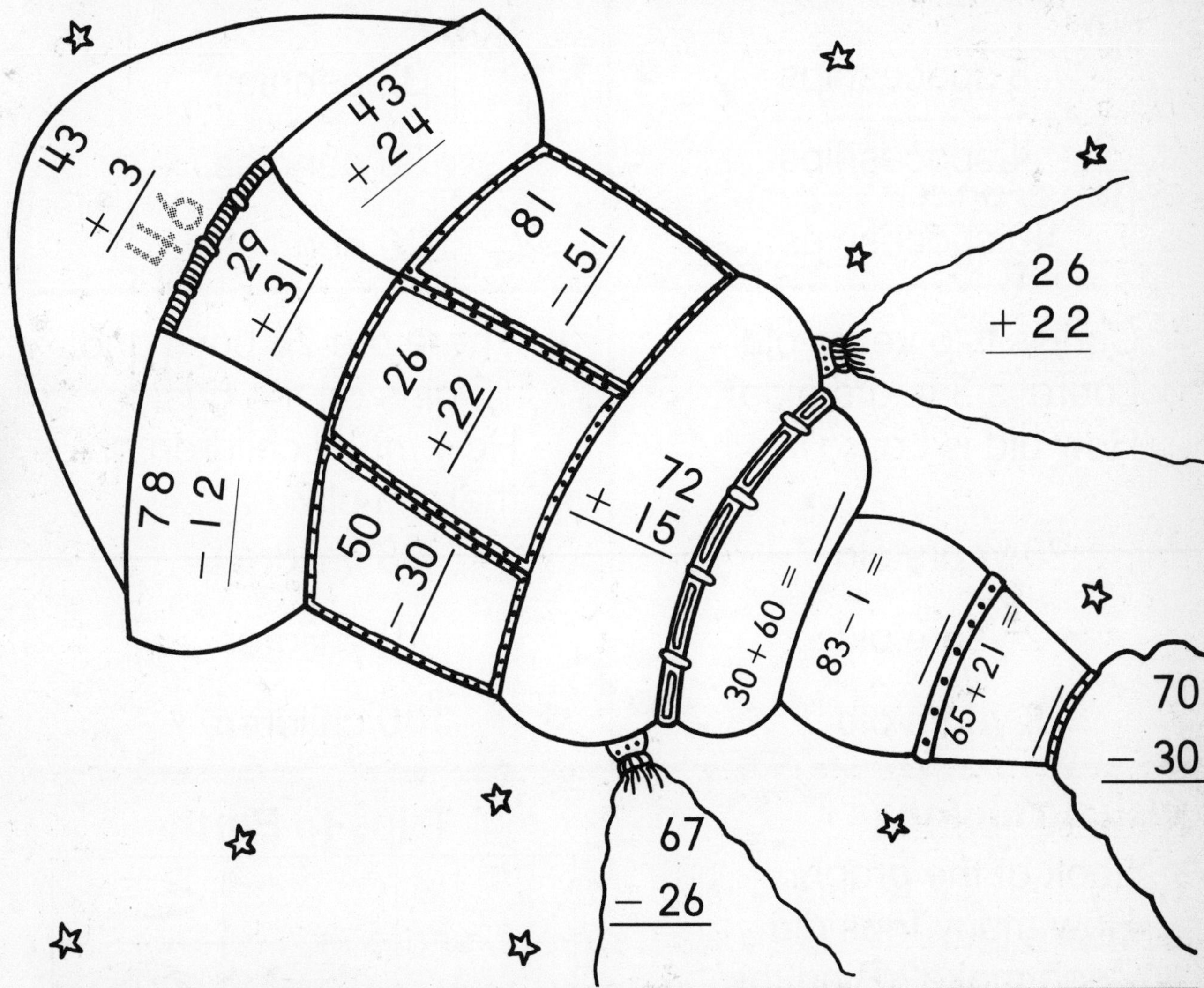

Number Sense

Ring the one you think will have the greatest sum or difference.

1. $65 + 23$ $35 + 23$ $15 + 23$

2. $67 - 15$ $67 - 25$ $67 - 5$

Name ____

11.10

USE WHAT YOU KNOW

Problem Solving

Find the Reasonable Answer

Ring the answer that makes sense.

1. Miguel had 6 spaceships.
He lost 2.
How many does he have now?

8 spaceships

4 spaceships

40 spaceships

2. Pete had 44 pennies.
He gave Sue 12.
How many does he have now?

32 pennies

56 pennies

320 pennies

3. Corliss is 5 years old.
Laura is 3 years older.
How old is Laura?

20 years old

2 years old

8 years old

4. There are 26 boys and 12 girls on the bus.
How many children are there in all?

38 children

14 children

140 children

Visual Thinking

5. Look at the graph.
How many trips did Zeeb make? Ring the answer that makes sense.

2 trips

30 trips

300 trips

Trips to Earth

Jath	Zeeb	Lork
		spaceship
	spaceship	spaceship
	spaceship	spaceship
spaceship	spaceship	spaceship

1 spaceship means 10 trips.

Use with text pages 373–374.

Name ______________________________

Problem-Solving Strategy

Use Estimation

Ring the better estimate.
Then find the exact answer.
You may use a calculator.

1. Ben buys these things.

 32¢

 53¢

About how much money did Ben spend?

about 70¢

about 80¢

Exact answer  ______ ¢

---

2. Jen has 78¢.
She buys goggles for 55¢.
About how much money does Jen have left?

about 20¢

about 30¢

Exact answer ______ ¢

---

3. Len has 96¢.
He buys a  for 62¢.
About how much money does Len have left?

about 50¢

about 30¢

Exact answer ______ ¢

Story Corner

4. Make up a story problem about this picture. Give it to a friend to solve.

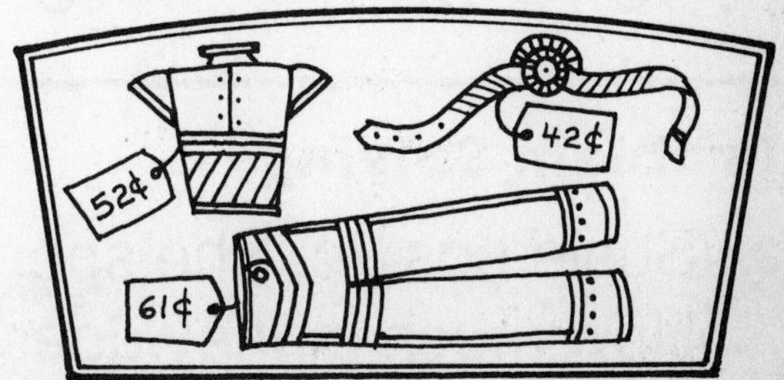

Name ______________________________

12.1
USE WHAT YOU KNOW

Sums and Differences

Tell a story about the pennies.
Add or subtract.

1.

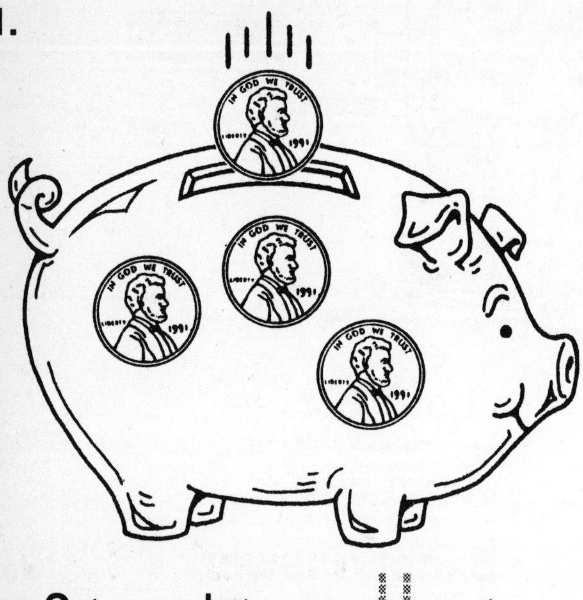

3¢ + 1¢ = __4__ ¢

4¢ − 1¢ = __3__ ¢

2.

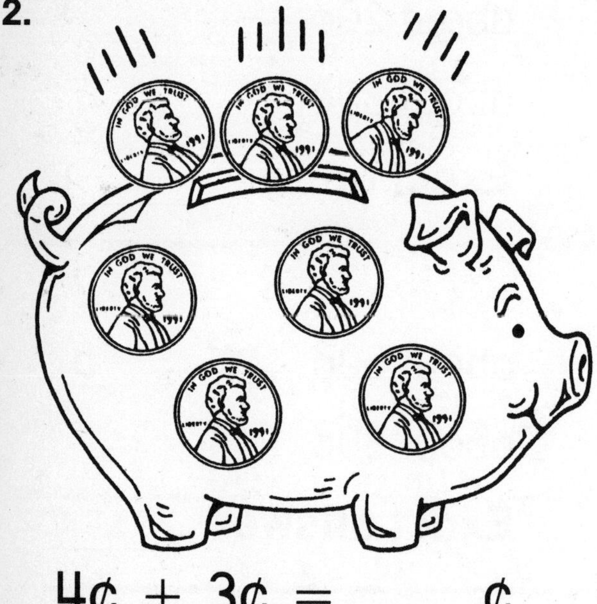

4¢ + 3¢ = _____ ¢

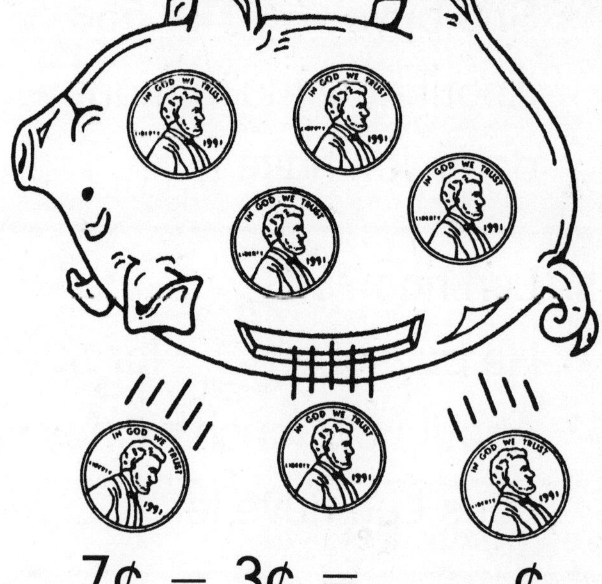

7¢ − 3¢ = _____ ¢

Problem Solving

3. Susie has 9¢. She spends 2¢.
How much money does she have left? _____ ¢

Use with text pages 385–386.

Name ____________________

12.2 USE WHAT YOU KNOW

Using Doubles

Add or subtract. Use counters.

1.	$1 + 1 = 2$	$2 - 1 = 1$	$2 + 2$	$4 - 2$	$3 + 3$	$6 - 3$
2.	$4 + 4$	$8 - 4$	$5 + 5$	$10 - 5$	$6 + 6$	$12 - 6$

Number Sense

Try these in your head.

3.	$7 + 7$	$14 - 7$	$8 + 8$	$16 - 8$	$9 + 9$	$18 - 9$

Name ____________________

12.3 USE WHAT YOU KNOW

Doubles Plus One

Do these in your head. Then write the sums.

1. 1 + 1 = 2, so 1 + 2 = 3.

2. 4 + 4 = 8, so 4 + 5 = ____.

3. 0 + 0 = 0, so 0 + 1 = ____.

Write the sums.

4. 8 + 8 = ____, so 8 + 9 = ____.

5. 7 + 7 = ____, so 7 + 8 = ____.

Look for doubles to find the sums.

6. $\begin{array}{r} 5 \\ +\ 5 \\ \hline \end{array}$ $\begin{array}{r} 3 \\ +\ 3 \\ \hline \end{array}$ $\begin{array}{r} 6 \\ +\ 7 \\ \hline \end{array}$ $\begin{array}{r} 4 \\ +\ 5 \\ \hline \end{array}$ $\begin{array}{r} 2 \\ +\ 2 \\ \hline \end{array}$ $\begin{array}{r} 3 \\ +\ 4 \\ \hline \end{array}$

7. $\begin{array}{r} 2 \\ +\ 3 \\ \hline \end{array}$ $\begin{array}{r} 8 \\ +\ 8 \\ \hline \end{array}$ $\begin{array}{r} 5 \\ +\ 6 \\ \hline \end{array}$ $\begin{array}{r} 8 \\ +\ 9 \\ \hline \end{array}$ $\begin{array}{r} 4 \\ +\ 4 \\ \hline \end{array}$ $\begin{array}{r} 6 \\ +\ 6 \\ \hline \end{array}$

Reasoning

Write the sums.

8. 5 + 5 = 10,
so 5 + 6 = ____.

9. 6 + 6 = 12,
so 6 + 7 = ____.

Use with text pages 389–390.

Name ____________________

Doubles Minus One

Do these in your head. Then write the sums.

1. 4 + 4 = 8, so 4 + 3 = 7.
2. 7 + 7 = 14, so 7 + 6 = ____.
3. 8 + 8 = 16, so 8 + 7 = ____.
4. 9 + 9 = 18, so 9 + 8 = ____.
5. 6 + 6 = 12, so 6 + 5 = ____.

Look for doubles to find the sums.

6. $\begin{array}{r} 9 \\ +\ 9 \\ \hline \end{array}$ $\begin{array}{r} 7 \\ +\ 6 \\ \hline \end{array}$ $\begin{array}{r} 4 \\ +\ 3 \\ \hline \end{array}$ $\begin{array}{r} 1 \\ +\ 1 \\ \hline \end{array}$ $\begin{array}{r} 9 \\ +\ 8 \\ \hline \end{array}$ $\begin{array}{r} 7 \\ +\ 7 \\ \hline \end{array}$

7. $\begin{array}{r} 8 \\ +\ 8 \\ \hline \end{array}$ $\begin{array}{r} 1 \\ +\ 0 \\ \hline \end{array}$ $\begin{array}{r} 5 \\ +\ 4 \\ \hline \end{array}$ $\begin{array}{r} 8 \\ +\ 7 \\ \hline \end{array}$ $\begin{array}{r} 4 \\ +\ 4 \\ \hline \end{array}$ $\begin{array}{r} 5 \\ +\ 5 \\ \hline \end{array}$

Number Sense

8. Ring 5 + 5 red.
Ring 5 + 4 blue.
Ring 5 + 6 green.

Use with text pages 391–392.

Name ____________________

Make a 10

Use counters and the 10-frame.
Start with the greater number. Make a 10. Then add.

1.	7 + 4 11	8 + 6	3 + 9	4 + 8	5 + 9	9 + 4
2.	9 + 6	3 + 8	7 + 5	2 + 9	5 + 8	9 + 7
3.	6 + 8	4 + 9	7 + 9	4 + 7	8 + 3	5 + 7

Number Sense

Do these in your head.
Make a 10. Write how many extra.

4. $2 + 9 = 10 +$ ____ extra

5. $7 + 5 = 10 +$ ____ extra

Use with text pages 393–394.

Name ______________________________

Adding Three Numbers

Use a spinner.
Spin. Write the number in the box.

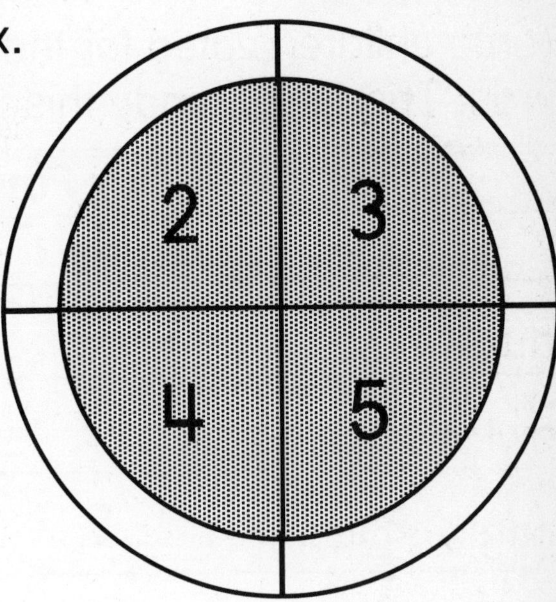

1.

2	6	5
2	4	5
+ ☐	+ ☐	+ ☐

2.

3	4	1
7	4	9
+ ☐	+ ☐	+ ☐

3.

2	1	8	3	6	7
8	1	2	3	6	3
+ ☐	+ ☐	+ ☐	+ ☐	+ ☐	+ ☐

Reasoning

Ring the one in each pair that you think has the greater sum. Then solve to check.

4.

7	8
3	2
+ 6	+ 5

5.

4	3
4	4
+ 2	+ 4

Name ________________________________

12.7
USE WHAT YOU KNOW

Problem-Solving Strategy

Make a Table

Some children voted for their favorite birds. Then they made this table.

Our Favorite Birds			
	Grade 1	Grade 2	Grade 3
duck	10	7	3
owl	12	13	7
eagle	9	8	15

Read the table. Answer these questions about it.

1. How many children in Grade 1 like ducks best? 10 children
2. How many children in Grade 2 like owls best? _____ children
3. How many children in Grade 3 like eagles best? _____ children
4. How many children in all like ducks best? _____ children

Story Corner

5. Write a question about the table. Give it to a classmate to answer.

____

____

Use with text pages 397–398.

Name ______________________________

Sums and Differences to 14

Write the addition facts that help.
Then complete the subtraction facts.

1. 12 − 5 = 7 | 7 + 5 = 12
   14 − 5
   10 − 6

2. 9 − 3
   13 − 8
   11 − 4
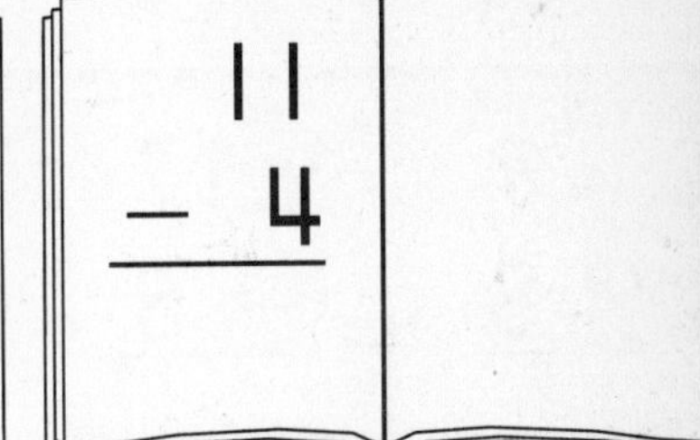

3. 12 − 8
   14 − 7
   13 − 6

4. 11 − 9
   8 − 6
   14 − 8

Problem Solving

5. Jon filled 4 bags with leaves. His mother filled 5 bags. How many bags in all did they fill?

   ______ bags

6. Mollie washed 12 glasses. Her brother washed 6 glasses. How many more glasses did Mollie wash?

   ______ more glasses

Use with text pages 401–402.

Name ____________________

12.9 USE WHAT YOU KNOW

Sums and Differences to 18

Write the sum and difference for each pair.

1.

4	12	8	16	8	13
+ 8	− 8	+ 8	− 8	+ 5	− 5
12	4				

2.

9	17	7	15	2	11
+ 8	− 8	+ 8	− 8	+ 9	− 9

3.

7	14	6	15	9	18
+ 7	− 7	+ 9	− 9	+ 9	− 9

Reasoning

Which way would you use to find each sum? Draw a line to match.

4. $9 + 7 = ?$ • • Add doubles.
5. $9 + 2 = ?$ • • Count on.
6. $6 + 6 = ?$ • • Make a 10.

Use with text pages 403–404.

Name ______________________________

12.10
USE WHAT YOU KNOW

Fact Families

Write each fact family.

1. 6, 7, 13

6 + 7 = 13 | 7 + 6 = 13
13 − 7 = 6 | 13 − 6 = 7

2. 

___ + ___ = ___ | ___ + ___ = ___
___ − ___ = ___ | ___ − ___ = ___

3. 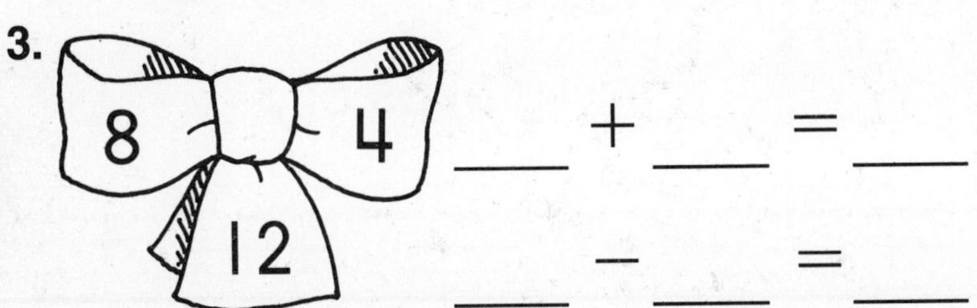

___ + ___ = ___ | ___ + ___ = ___
___ − ___ = ___ | ___ − ___ = ___

4. 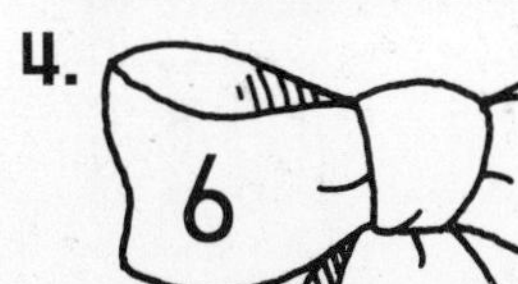

___ + ___ = ___ | ___ + ___ = ___
___ − ___ = ___ | ___ − ___ = ___

Number Sense

5. Ring an estimate. Then use a 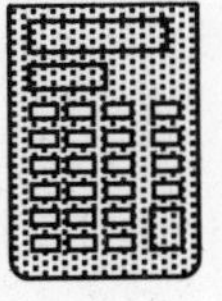 to solve.

There are 9 children swimming.
8 more come.
Then 10 of them leave.
How many children are swimming?

more than 9

fewer than 9

_____ children

Name ______________________________

12.11 USE WHAT YOU KNOW

Making Equal Groups

Write how many groups.
Then write the addition sentence.

1.  

2 groups of 1

1 + 1 = 2

____ groups of 2

____ + ____ + ____ = ____

2. 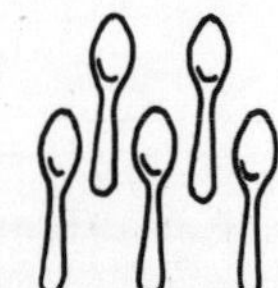 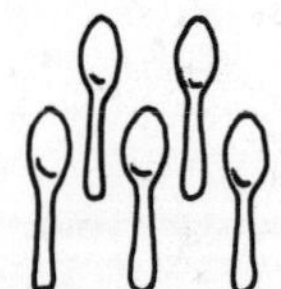

____ groups of 5

____ + ____ + ____ = ____

____ groups of 3

____ + ____ = ____

3.  

____ groups of 2

____ + ____ = ____

____ groups of 4

____ + ____ + ____ = ____

Reasoning

4. Ring the child who has more stones.

Use with text pages 407–408.

Name ______________________________

12.12
USE WHAT YOU KNOW

Problem-Solving Strategy

Make a Model

Work with a group.
Use counters to model each problem.
Give an equal number to each child in the group.
Write how many counters each child gets.

1. There are 8 toy cars. There are 4 children. How many toy cars does each child get? Each child gets 2 cars.

2. There are 6 blocks. There are 2 children. How many blocks does each child get? Each child gets _____ blocks.

3. There are 12 books. There are 3 children. How many books does each child get? Each child gets _____ books.

4. There are 15 crayons. There are 5 children. How many crayons does each child get? Each child gets _____ crayons

Reasoning

5. Ring the child who has fewer shells.

Name ______________________________

Tallying Events

Work with a friend.
Use a pencil and a paper clip to make a spinner. Predict which color the spinner will stop on most often. Ring the color.

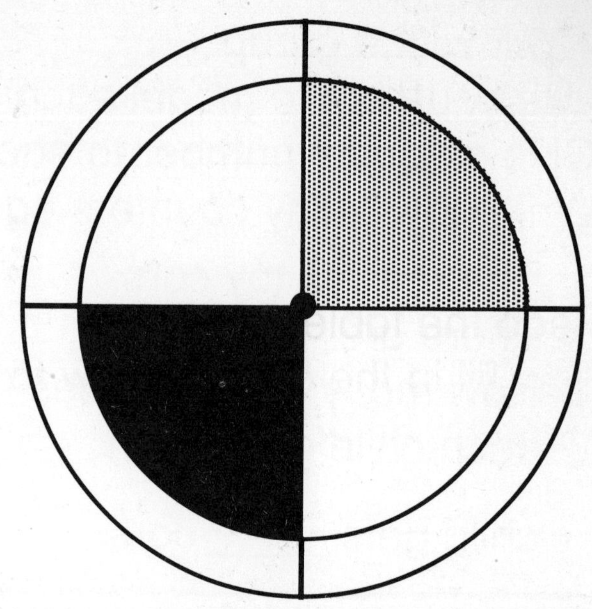

gray black white

Try it. Take turns spinning the paper clip. Spin 10 times. Make a tally mark after each spin.

	Tally Marks	Total
gray		
black		
white		

Reasoning

Raymond and a friend took turns spinning a spinner. The spinner stopped on blue 3 times. It stopped on red 7 times. Draw and color what you think the spinner looked like.

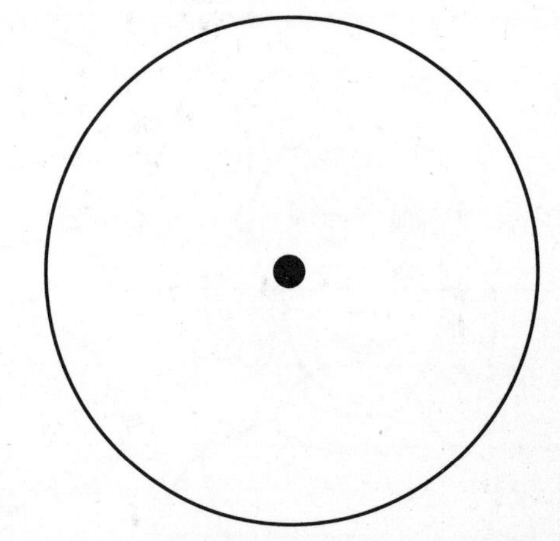

Use with text pages 411–412.

Name ____________________

Graphing Data

○	𝍸
△	𝍸 |||
□	|||

Read the table.
Now fill in the graph below to show how many times each shape was picked.

Color Graph

○										
△										
□										
	0	1	2	3	4	5	6	7	8	9	10

2. Which shape was picked most often? ____________

3. How many picks were made in all? _____ picks

Story Corner

4. Write a question about the graph.
   Give it to a friend to answer.

Name ______________________________

12.15
USE WHAT YOU KNOW

Problem Solving

Choose the Strategy

Draw a picture or use counters to solve.

1. There are 12 oranges. There are 3 trees. Each tree has an equal number of oranges on it. How many oranges are on each tree?

   There are __4__ oranges on each tree.

2. There are 5 ears of corn in the brown bag. There are 7 ears of corn in the white bag. How many ears of corn are in both bags?

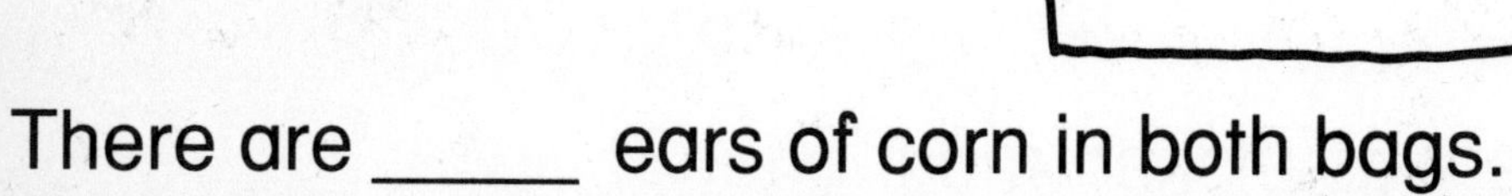

   There are _____ ears of corn in both bags.

3. Lindy had 17 grapes. She ate 8 of them. How many grapes does Lindy have left?

   Lindy has _____ grapes left.

Number Sense

4. Ring the better estimate. There are 2 groups of 4 birds. One group flies away. How many birds are left?

   more than 8

   fewer than 8

Use with text pages 415–416.